PRAISE FOR *BREAKING INTO VENTURE*

This book is a GPS for outsiders seeking to get their bearings in the venture capital industry. Rich with examples and tips, it demystifies the venture capital industry for the novice and is a must-read for anyone seeking an adventure in venture capital.

> —**HAYAGREEVA RAO**, Atholl McBean Professor of Organizational Behavior, Graduate School of Business, Stanford University and *Wall Street Journal* bestselling coauthor of *Scaling Up Excellence*

I never understood the full meaning of 'venture capital' until reading Allison's honest account of what it takes to identify and invest in transformative businesses long before they become household names. Whether you're trying to build a new company or put your own capital to better use, this book contains countless pillars of professional wisdom.

> —**MICHAEL KOENIGS**, executive producer at Disney-ABC and host of ABC's *More in Common*

In a bold act of democratizing access to one of the most enigmatic but influential corners of our economy, Baum Gates brings us a remarkable and delightful insider's guide to venture capital. A must-read for anyone interested in working in, investing in, or understanding technology and the forces driving its development.

> —**DIANE GHERSON**, senior lecturer at Harvard Business School, independent director, and former CHRO of IBM

The mission of this book is to make it easier for people with new and different perspectives to find their way in a historically exclusive and homogeneous industry. Allison breaks down complex and opaque concepts in a way that is accessible to anyone. Whether you are trying to break into the industry or just understand this important asset class, this book is a great resource.

—**ANGELA LEE**, professor of venture capital at Columbia Business School and founder of 37 Angels

The inner workings of venture capital can be ambiguous and complex. This book demystifies the industry powering the technology behind our everyday lives and equips the reader with principles that can apply to anyone looking to invest, raise money for a new idea, or build a career in technology.

—**MALA SINGH**, Chief People Officer, Electronic Arts

BREAKING
INTO
VENTURE

BREAKING
INTO
VENTURE

**An Outsider Turned Venture Capitalist
Shares How to Take Risks, Create Power, and
Build Life-Changing Wealth**

ALLISON BAUM GATES

NEW YORK   CHICAGO   SAN FRANCISCO   ATHENS   LONDON
MADRID   MEXICO CITY   MILAN   NEW DELHI
SINGAPORE   SYDNEY   TORONTO

1 2 3 4 5 6 7 8 9   LCR   28 27 26 25 24 23

ISBN   978-1-264-69894-3
MHID   1-264-69894-1

e-ISBN   978-1-264-70268-8
e-MHID   1-264-70268-X

This publication is designed to provide accurate and authoritative information in regard to the subject matter covered. It is sold with the understanding that neither the author nor the publisher is engaged in rendering legal, accounting, securities trading, or other professional services. If legal advice or other expert assistance is required, the services of a competent professional person should be sought.
—*From a Declaration of Principles Jointly Adopted by a Committee of the American Bar Association and a Committee of Publishers and Associations*

In some cases, the author created fictional companies and characters to illustrate her points. Names, characters, business, events, and incidents are the products of the author's imagination. Any resemblance to actual persons, living or dead, or actual events is purely coincidental.

McGraw Hill books are available at special quantity discounts to use as premiums and sales promotions or for use in corporate training programs. To contact a representative, please visit the Contact Us pages at www.mhprofessional.com.

McGraw Hill is committed to making our products accessible to all learners. To learn more about the available support and accommodations we offer, please contact us at accessibility@mheducation.com. We also participate in the Access Text Network (www.accesstext.org), and ATN members may submit requests through ATN.

To the next generation of investors

CONTENTS

PART THREE

ADD VALUE

INTRODUCTION

When I was a little girl, I had widely varying career aspirations. Briefly enamored by the cuteness of little animals, I had a veterinarian phase, but mostly I wanted to be some variation of a writer. I self-published my first book from underneath the kitchen table by the ripe old age of six, culminating in a self-crayon-illustrated fiction series called *Dixie the Aardvark*, which chronicled the misadventures of an overweight aardvark and her best friend, Missy the Chicken. I spent my summers at journalism camp learning to write leads. In middle school, I even tried on the emo poet thing for size. I religiously chronicled all these ambitions in my journal, which I named "Buddy," hoping that one day the journal itself might even become source material (I assure you, it has not).

However, once I started to internalize the concept of money, then power, then influence, I worried that writers might not have enough of these things, so I shifted my aspirations toward being president of the United States. Disappointed by the fact that you cannot be president until you are 35, I thought I'd better keep myself busy and earn some cash in the meantime. So, I started a variety of businesses, ranging from jewelry (beaded chokers, specifically) to dog washing to custom novelty pillows that I sewed at home on my grandma's Singer sewing machine. I would prefer not to totally bore you on page one with the full rundown of my winding path of endless curiosities, but suffice it to say that *never* at one single moment did I *ever* stop and think, "I'd really like to be a venture capitalist."

In fact, the first time I even heard of venture capital, I was in my early twenties, and I was embarking on a career on Wall Street. I did not know what exactly venture capital was, but I had learned that my ex-boyfriend whom I had just broken up with, largely due to his extended status as unemployed and seeming lack of career ambition, had been invited to join a venture capital firm started by his billionaire fraternity brother. This was unremarkable to me, until I learned that they had invested in a social media company called Instagram that everyone was talking about as the next big thing. The company was subsequently bought by Facebook for $1 billion.[1] I did not know how much my ex had benefited personally from this sale, but the fact that in a matter of weeks he went from hanging around at my apartment all day to a being successful venture capitalist (VC) filled me with envy. How could he be so lucky?

It would be several years before I found my own pathway into venture capital, but I suddenly had a new awareness of this mysterious industry that seemed to have its tentacles in every aspect of our daily lives. You may be thinking, "Venture capital seems cool, but it has nothing to do with me," or "I've seen some pitches on *Shark Tank*, but I could never be an investor," or "I don't know anything about venture capital." However, whether you like it or not, venture capitalists know about you, and we are investing in new technology that is changing the way you watch TV, search the internet, find your future partner, or drive your car. Not only that, we're investing in the technology that your doctors use to store and analyze your health information, or track your pregnancy. We're investing in the technology that your employer uses to hire you, pay you, and measure your performance. Technology is changing everything about the world around us, and venture capital is fueling the next generation of influential innovations.

In addition to shaping the fabric of the world around us, venture capital investing is creating a life-changing amount of wealth for its constituents. According to a recent survey, the median cash compensation for a partner at a venture capital firm was more than $900,000 per year.[2] Salary plus bonuses for venture capital associates, who are typically only a few years out of school, reached $196,000.[3] However, the lion's share of earnings for venture capitalists comes from the payouts from their successful investments. In the last few years, venture capital has outperformed every other asset class globally,[4] returning as much as $659 billion to its investors and employees over the course of one year.[5] To put that in perspective, that is more than the annual nominal GDP of Taiwan,[6] a country of 24 million people. However, instead of venture capital returns getting distributed to *millions* of people, they are distributed to *thousands* of people. In fact, a typical venture capital firm has less than 100 investors and fewer than 15 employees.[7]

Despite all this wealth and glory, most of the successful venture capitalists I interviewed for this book also had very little insight into the industry before they became part of it. I can't count the number of times I heard, "I didn't know what a venture capitalist was until I was on the path to become one." They told me, "I never saw myself as a VC," or "I had heard of venture investors, but it never occurred to me that I could be one." I found myself wondering, how is it possible that an industry with so much money, power, and influence could be so under the radar?

WHAT IS VENTURE CAPITAL, AND WHY IS IT SO MYSTERIOUS?

Venture capital is a form of *private equity financing*. It is a form of *financing* because it provides the money that makes a new business or venture possible. It is considered to be *equity* investing because investors trade money for a percentage ownership stake in a business. As equity owners, the investors can potentially lose all their capital, but if the business is successful, they will share in the profits. Because there is no limit to how big a company can grow, potential returns for equity investors are also unlimited. By contrast, *debt* financing is when investors lend money to a business with the expectation of full repayment plus an interest rate. Debt investors are far less likely to lose all their capital, but the potential upside is limited.

Venture capital is considered *private*, because it does not happen on a public, listed exchange, but instead as a direct transaction between two parties (and most likely, a bunch of lawyers). In a private transaction, the only information available to anyone else is whatever the involved parties are willing to share, and there are no standardized methods of ensuring the information being shared is accurate. As a result, private equity investing can be very risky for anyone without the experience, networks, or direct knowledge of the new businesses they are funding, the people building them, or the technologies they are promising to create.

In an effort to protect people from making stupid mistakes investing in an industry with a high likelihood of failure and no standardized information sharing, the government strictly regulated who was allowed to make private equity investments and instead provided public funding for innovation and new technology development. However, everything changed in 1946, when the innovation of the atomic bomb led to the end of World War II and solidified the fact that superior technology was not just a "nice to have" but actually a critical factor in national security. All of a sudden, the government had a clear motivation to incentivize even more investment in research and development of new technology for military uses, so it started offering large grants to public and private institutions (primarily universities) to work on whatever could save the world next.

Around the same time, a man named Frederick Terman returned from the war to a role as the dean of the School of Engineering at Stanford University. He saw an opportunity to attract these lucrative research grants from the Department of Defense, so he aggressively expanded the university's science and engineering departments with a specific focus on developing new, innovative technology. In

1951, Terman established the Stanford Industrial Park where he leased university real estate to high-tech firms like Lockheed Martin, Hewlett-Packard, and others who may have wanted access to the patented technology being developed at the school.[8] Many consider this to be the birth of Silicon Valley as the center of the technology innovation and venture capital universe, as it is commonly seen today.[9]

The richest families in America were watching what was happening at these universities, and they started to see an opportunity to gain access to this innovative technology and sell it for use beyond just the military. The Rockefellers, the Vanderbilts, and the Whitneys all used their family wealth to invest in innovative new ideas and bring them to market. Georges Doriot, a professor at Harvard Business School, and two other partners started the first venture capital fund in 1946, called the American Research and Development Corporation (ARDC). They demonstrated the power of venture capital to their investors when they put $70,000 into a company called Digital Equipment Company in 1957. Fourteen years later, their investment was worth more than $355 million, solidifying that financing innovative technology businesses could prove incredibly lucrative for risk-loving investors as well.[10]

As the industry flourished over the next several decades, venture capitalists started to gain real and meaningful influence over which technology companies got off the ground. However, it was government regulators who held the keys to who had the ability to participate in the eventual profits. These regulators had to walk a fine line between incentivizing investment in the innovation that has made and kept America a dominant world power and making sure that investors were adequately protected from downside risks in an industry that is so challenging to understand and navigate. The desire to protect investors typically took precedent, limiting the asset class only to individuals with a lot of personal wealth or well-capitalized entities that could withstand significant losses if the investments were to go to zero.

Over time, as venture capital has grown in its success as well as its influence, major regulatory changes have been focused on democratizing access to venture capital as a critical funding source for entrepreneurs, but less so on democratizing access to the profits that the asset class generates. Recently, more attention has been called to the fact that keeping venture capital reserved for only the already wealthy has had an adverse effect on the types of entrepreneurs and businesses that those funds choose to back—venture capital investors fund businesses started by their already wealthy friends, and when the businesses succeed, the rich get richer, and it becomes even harder for anyone without money to break into the industry. The result has been a stunning lack of diversity in both venture capital itself and entrepreneurship and technology overall.

In recent years, policies have started to turn toward making venture capital more accessible, transparent, and accountable, and it has started to emerge as both a viable and desirable career pathway for aspiring professionals. However, in an industry that has historically operated on an apprenticeship model, formalized pathways for learning how to get your foot in the door or figuring out how to succeed once you're there are few and far between. That needs to change. If we want technology to lead to a better world for everyone, if we want technology to live up to its promise of democratizing information, resources, and opportunities, we need all types of people involved in the process of building it. Building investment firms that look like the user base of the companies they are funding will only be possible if we truly lift the veil, explain the real incentives that drive how venture capital works, and provide tangible tools and tactics for how to break in, stay in, and thrive. That is what I am here to do.

Maybe you don't care about changing the world through venture capital, and that's completely okay, too. You may be interested in the industry for other reasons. Even though it wasn't on my list of childhood aspirations, being a venture capitalist is also, in my opinion, the best job in the world. I get to spend my days meeting with intelligent, passionate entrepreneurs. I get to follow my sense of endless curiosity, choose who I work with (mostly), and play a role in imagining and building the future. Not only that, if you are good at it, you have the chance to build life-changing wealth. There is no limit to how much money you can make. If I had known this was a real job when I was younger, I would have started down this path sooner. But then again, if I had known how hard it would be to find my way in as an outsider, I also might not have tried at all. This book is designed to make sure that doesn't happen to you.

MY PATHWAY INTO VENTURE

One of the reasons I am so confident that you can find your way in venture capital is because I did, and without anyone guiding me. I did not go to business school. I did not start or work at a big, famous technology company. I did not come from a wealthy family. I did not plan on becoming a venture capitalist, partially because I didn't believe it was possible for me, and partially because I didn't know very much about it.

Growing up in the Midwest, venture capital was never something I heard or cared about. Like many people, I was primarily focused on how to avoid becoming my parents. I loved them more than anything, but I watched both of their careers being constantly disrupted by technology, and it was a constant source of financial and emotional strain for them, their marriage, and our family. So I dedicated the first two decades of my life to doing everything I could to make sure it didn't happen to me.

I woke up at 5:03 a.m. every day of high school to squeeze in a workout and finish my homework before heading to club meetings, sports practices, and a string of honors classes. I got into Harvard, I hustled my way to an internship at Goldman Sachs, where I endured footballs thrown past my head and a culture where high-strung men were either yelling at me or trying to make out with me. I endured brutally early mornings getting everyone's obnoxiously specific coffee order just right, seemingly endless nights entertaining clients, and a nagging feeling that whatever I was doing was never enough.

I thought I was doing everything right, but the financial crisis of 2008 forced every business into survival mode, and even formerly lucrative roles on the trading floor were being replaced by algorithms. The pathway I had envisioned for myself—working hard to earn a lot of money very early in my career—was not really an option anymore. Paychecks were cut significantly, many entry-level roles were automated, and a demand for more transparency in financial markets meant that margins were being squeezed and looming regulation created a culture of fear. Technology was being used to monitor employee conversations to flag potential compliance issues, and even a colloquial abbreviation of a vulgar word used in an email or chat was flagged to our superiors. How could it possibly be that despite my lifelong dedication to avoiding disruption from technology, it was happening all around me? And not only that, but it was only a few short years after graduating from one of the best universities in the world? If this was a problem for my parents, and for me, it was surely going to be a problem for every working adult in America.

I decided I'd much rather be on the side of the disruptor (in this case, technology), instead of the side of the disrupted (in this case, the finance industry), so I set my sights on getting a job at a technology company. It was an exciting time as Google and Facebook had only recently opened New York outposts, and there was a burgeoning local startup scene emerging under the ridiculous name of Silicon Alley. I searched local job boards, asked all my friends outside of finance, and started applying for whatever roles seemed to be a fit for my skill set. Unfortunately, the intersection between technology jobs, my economics degree, and my experience trading equity derivatives was very slim. I still remember the stunning silence on the other end of the phone call with a recruiter when I told her I wanted to work at Zocdoc, a quickly growing technology startup designed to bring transparency to the process of finding a doctor. She finally spoke up, though I wish she hadn't, because she said something to the effect of, "Honestly, I'm just not sure what you would do here."

To say this was frustrating is an understatement. I was disappointed, disillusioned, and lost. My self-confidence was battered; I couldn't figure out what to do next. Worse, I was still trudging to the trading floor every morning, feeling guilty about my lack of gratitude for the opportunity ahead of me. I was still searching for ways to break into tech, so I started working on projects and attending events related to startups, and I came across a job opportunity at a new startup called General Assembly. It had started as one of the first coworking spaces in New York City, and its founders noticed that most of the startups working out of the space were desperate to hire employees with technology skills, but they couldn't find them, even though unemployment in New York and the United States overall was at record highs at the time.

So the team decided to stop looking for tech talent and start making it instead. General Assembly launched classes and bootcamps to train working professionals—like me, like my parents, like you—in the skills they needed to pursue technology jobs that they actually loved: things like web development, digital marketing, product management, and user experience design. When I interviewed for the job, I emphasized that I might not know anything about these skill sets, and I didn't know much about education either, but I was passionate about the problem they were solving because it was *my* problem.

Somehow, my passion convinced the founders to bring me on as one of their first employees focused on the budding education business. In a matter of days, I quit my once coveted job on Wall Street, my salary dropped by more than 50 percent, and I was the happiest I had ever been. It didn't even matter that I couldn't pay the rent on my Tribeca apartment anymore and had to move into my boyfriend's parents' house on Long Island. I was having a blast and making a difference in the world. Not only was I no longer part of the problem, I was building the solution. We were growing at breakneck speed, touching hundreds and then thousands of lives, and I felt invincible. How could I have been so wrong as to trudge along in my initial career path in finance when something this exhilarating was possible?

Less than a year later, I moved to Hong Kong to set up our business in Asia. By that time, I had run hundreds, if not thousands of classes for working professionals on things like coding fundamentals, establishing a business entity, effective Facebook marketing, brand building, and pitching your startup. Our most popular class of all, however, was "Introduction to Angel Investing." We sold out class after class, even after I raised prices, added additional time slots, and found larger venues. I knew there was something more to do here, and it was interesting to me that more people were interested in investing in startups than in building them.

Eager to capitalize on this seemingly insatiable demand, I approached Tytus Michalski, the angel investor whom I had recruited to teach these classes, and I pitched him on building a more comprehensive education program together. Could we turn this into a full course, instead of a one-time class? I told him it would cost him nothing and we could split the profits 50/50, although General Assembly would maintain ownership of the content we developed. After pretending to consider my proposition, he came back with one of his own.

We met at a Starbucks tucked below a cobblestone staircase on Duddell Street in Hong Kong. I sipped my coffee and leaned forward in my chair, excited to hear what he had to say. He told me he was not interested in teaching more angel investors, but he had begun the process of starting his own venture capital fund and wanted me to join him as his partner. I was totally blindsided. Did he have the right person? How could I possibly be an investor when the only things I knew about angel investing I had learned from his class?

He insisted that, in fact, I knew more about venture capital than I realized. When setting up new classes at General Assembly, my priority was to recruit amazing teachers. That meant that first and foremost, I was combing the entire world to find people that were absolutely amazing at what they were doing in technology—whether that was building products, running marketing campaigns, hiring teams, or raising money—and were passionate enough to want to share their talent with other people. Then, I had to filter for the teachers with strong brands and personal networks so they could tap into their existing audience as potential students. Finally, I had to convince them to come work with me instead of doing it on their own. That, Tytus insisted, was really what being a venture capitalist was all about.

With that, I took a gigantic leap of faith and joined Tytus to build Fresco Capital, a global seed fund investing at the intersection of people and technology. We went on to raise tens of millions of dollars, Stephen Forte joined us as our third partner, and we invested in more than 70 companies, some of which have grown into billion-dollar businesses. I continued to call Asia my home, first Hong Kong and then Tokyo, though I spent the better part of six years living on an airplane traveling to meet investors, founders, and influencers all around the region and the world. During that time, I grew passionate about changing the way the venture capital industry worked, but I feared I didn't fully understand it myself. I wanted more traditional experience in venture, and I wanted to be at the epicenter of the innovation ecosystem, so I left my life in Japan and bought a one-way ticket to San Francisco.

I joined a storied firm on Sand Hill Road, Trinity Ventures, which had been investing in venture capital for over 30 years and promised to teach me how Silicon Valley *really* works. Caught in the crosshairs of a rapidly changing industry, however, the firm found itself growing less and less competitive versus larger firms with big teams who could add tangible value to businesses to help them grow faster. They were also losing versus specialized firms with deeper sector knowledge to inform their investments and unique expertise to help them grow. I wanted more of a focus and more of a competitive edge, so I went back to my entrepreneurial roots at another upstart fund called SemperVirens, where I am a general partner investing exclusively in B2B businesses changing the future of work through workforce technology, healthcare technology, and financial technology.

In addition to capital to invest, we have an extensive ecosystem of thousands of potential customers for our portfolio companies. The customers include the country's largest employers, insurance companies, and other distribution partners that can help accelerate go-to-market for new and innovative products and services. We leverage this platform of end buyers for sourcing innovations that are gaining traction, for diligence when we are evaluating whether a product or business has legs, to demonstrate our ability to add value when deals are competitive, and to help accelerate sales after we have invested to improve the odds of our investments' success. We embody a new model of venture whereby specialized sector focus helps us make better investment decisions faster, and a concrete platform for adding value helps us win deals and influence outcomes in a meaningful way.

YOUR PATHWAY INTO VENTURE

As I have walked this path between entrepreneurship and venture capital, many have asked me, "What do I need to do to get into venture capital?" Programs designed for budding investors are often geared toward hard skills—the mechanics of a term sheet, how to structure a deal, or how to calculate the correct valuation for a company. Just like learning how to throw a perfect pitch without anyone explaining how to get on the baseball team, venture math is important to know, but it is not nearly enough. Where are the tryouts happening? What are the criteria used to select players? Who is making the decisions about how much they get paid? These are the questions that must be answered first.

Beginning with a quick and (hopefully) painless primer on what venture capital is, how it works, and the various roles within it, I will set you up for a deeper understanding of the fundamental principles that have served as my guide in one of the most complex and opaque industries in the world. It took me nearly a decade to distill what often felt like a haphazard comedy of errors into these nine principles for success. This book is a road map for breaking into venture. I look forward to sharing it with you.

FACTS AND FUNDAMENTALS

Whether you are an entrepreneur, aspiring investor, or regular *Shark Tank* viewer, the image you have of a venture capitalist (VC) probably consists of someone sitting behind a large table, listening intently (or half-listening while looking down at their phone) to someone pitching their idea for a new business or technology. They have a discerning look of skepticism plastered across their face, and they are full of questions about why this new concept will or won't work. After some consideration, they quickly decide "yes" or "no," and the business either gets funded or it doesn't.

While this isn't far from the truth—VCs typically listen to dozens of pitches per week and hundreds or even thousands per year and are always full of questions—there is a lot happening behind the curtain, including entire teams of people that play a role in how decisions get made, why, and what it means for everyone involved.

Let's start by outlining some of the key players and terms that are important to know before we dive into how to navigate the industry.

At some point, a few people get together and decide to start a **venture capital firm**. Like most entrepreneurs, they believe they have something differentiated to offer their customers, most likely in the form of their personal networks, knowledge set, and expertise. So they incorporate, give themselves a name (most likely something to do with trees, rocks, or hypergrowth), and build a mysterious website that contains little to no real information about who they are or what they do. This corporation that represents the fund is called the **general partner**, and the individuals that own equity in it are called general partners as well. Typically, they will appoint one or more of them to be a **managing partner**, who is charged with the leadership, organization, and administration of the firm.

Although having a company, website, and team is great, we all know that a new startup needs revenue to survive. Venture capital firms get their revenue from managing **venture capital funds**. A fund is formed as a **limited partnership**, which is a **closed-end investment vehicle**, meaning that it has a specific size, investment mandate, and life cycle that are determined at inception and cannot change after they have been written up by a bunch of lawyers in documents and agreed to by all of the investors, who are called **limited partners**. "Limited" because they have limited control and limited liability over how the funds are used. Their losses are capped by the amount of money they put into the fund, and the proceeds from investments are shared according to the overall percentage of the fund that they have invested.

Not everyone can become a limited partner, as the government limits the ability to invest in venture capital funds to accredited investors, or people that have more than $1 million in assets or have made $200,000 per year for the last several years.[1] More recently, the US Securities and Exchange Commission (SEC) has loosened the restrictions to allow employees of funds or licensed finance professionals to invest as well. While there are some individuals that invest in venture capital funds, most limited partners are large institutional allocators of capital that have billions of dollars under management, and they are putting millions or hundreds of millions toward venture capital. These limited partners include university endowments, pension funds, banks, family offices, corporations with strategic interest in investing in innovation, or ultra-high-net-worth individuals.

The **general partners** assume responsibility for managing the capital in the fund, and therefore assume some of the risks associated with the investments they are making. In return, they charge the limited partners a **management fee**, which is usually calculated as a 2 percent annual fee on the assets in the partnership. They use these fees to hire a team, open an office, do due diligence on potential investments, and pay for whatever other expenses are necessary to make money for their investors. In return for their hard work managing and deploying a fund, general partners also charge **carried interest**, which is usually equivalent to a 20 percent fee on any profits after they have returned all of the initial capital to investors. We'll talk about how these incentives impact how VCs think, act, and invest in Principle 5, "Money Matters."

Each fund has a **fund life**, which is typically 10 years. This means that at the end of 10 years, all assets are returned to limited partners according to their percentage ownership in the fund, even if those investments have not had a **liquidity event**, meaning a sale via merger or acquisition, bankruptcy, or an initial public offering. This is why most venture capitalists are looking for some sort of exit within 10 years of investing. This makes venture capital **long-term capital**, meaning investors don't expect an immediate return, but 10 years sure does go by quickly when you're building a startup.

Each fund also has a dedicated **initial investment period**, which is usually three or four years, which is when the fund is allowed to make new investments. After this initial investment period is over, the rest of the fund life is spent managing the portfolio and adding capital to existing investments in **follow-on financings**. This is important because it means that in order to continue generating revenue from management fees to run the firm, and to continue making new investments that increase the chances of eventually earning carried interest, general partners need to raise new funds every two to three years, something commonly referred to as a **fund cycle**. A decision to hire a new member of the team, or the decision to make a new investment, can be highly dependent on where the venture capital firm is in their fund cycle. Usually if you are early in a fund cycle, your odds of getting funded or hired are better, since there are several years of runway ahead. If you're late in a fund cycle and the initial investment period is over but a new fund hasn't been raised yet, the bar is significantly higher.

Whenever a company raises venture capital, they seek to raise a financing round by selling equity in their business. This means they are not obligated to repay the capital they raise, but their investors will share in the unlimited upside of their potential growth. They typically select one firm to be the **lead investor**, and together they negotiate **terms**, which are summarized in a **term sheet**. All of the other investors in the round are called **coinvestors**, or **following investors**, because they accept the terms negotiated by the lead investor. Even though terms can seem very boring, they are also incredibly important, so we'll thoroughly cover them in Principle 4.

On the side of the venture capital fund, negotiating and completing an investment can take as little as a few weeks. However, most investments are years in the making as investors seek to build long-term relationships with entrepreneurs before deciding to fund their businesses. The process of meeting entrepreneurs and evaluating new investments is often referred to as **deal flow**, and most investment firms treat this process similar to sales. There is a funnel, qualification criteria, and concrete steps required to complete a deal, which we'll take the time to unpack in Parts One and Two where we discuss the intricate process of gaining access to high-quality investments as well as how to properly analyze them and select where to deploy your capital. Finally, in Part Three, we'll talk about how investors add value to their portfolio companies, hoping to ultimately tip the odds in their own favor and increase their likelihood of returning capital to their limited partners.

Although venture capital becomes a lot more approachable once you understand the basics, its never-ending intrigue lies in the fact that it is a sophisticated asset class investing in the technology that is changing our world, while also changing rapidly itself. I learn something new about what I do every single day, and I am constantly asking, "Does it have to be done that way?" The answer is often, "Well, actually not really, but we just always have!" The more questions we ask, the more we can uncover new ways of thinking and investing. However, I aim to provide a framework and context here for how things have traditionally been done so that you can get a better understanding of the incentives at play in venture capital. Even if you don't agree with *why*, grasping the *what* and the *how* is an important first step.

HOW DO VENTURE CAPITALISTS WORK?

When I was first getting started in venture, I asked a general partner what milestones I had to reach in order to become a GP at a large, established fund. He told me that the pathway was simple: I just had to pass the *wheelbarrow test*. I looked at him inquisitively, and he elaborated that the *wheelbarrow test* meant that the other general partners must believe that if they gave you an empty wheelbarrow, you could figure out how to turn it into a wheelbarrow full of money. I paused, desperately trying to maintain a straight face, wondering if this should make sense to me. If you're confused, so was I. What does that even mean? And why a wheelbarrow?

This is precisely the type of adage that keeps venture capital mysterious and exclusive. Instead of trying to decipher vague gardening analogies, I went about finding my own framework for what it takes to make it in the industry. The purpose of this book is to break those criteria down into some more clarifying detail so that if you are just getting started, you know where to begin.

The following pages are anchored by the three things that a successful venture capitalist absolutely must do. I call these the 3 As because I love alliteration, and it also makes them easier to remember:

1. **ACCESS.** Consistently identify and gain access to promising investment opportunities. We will cover three principles governing this process in Part One.

2. **ANALYZE.** Efficiently and effectively analyze investment opportunities and choose which are the most likely to succeed in a big enough way to generate meaningful returns. We will cover three principles governing this process in Part Two.

3. **ADD VALUE.** Positively alter the trajectory of an investment by adding value to the business, and by extension increasing its odds of returning the fund. We will cover three principles governing this process in Part Three.

I would be remiss if I did not mention that there is a fourth A that is not the focus of this book, but is an essential part of both short-term and long-term viability in the industry, and that is the ability to **accumulate funds**. Raising money from limited partners for your fund enables you to deploy capital into promising investments. I share lessons learned from my experience fundraising over the years, but as long as you are able to access, analyze, and add value effectively, the ability to accumulate funds will naturally follow.

Ultimately, all these responsibilities fall on the general partner(s), but especially as fund sizes have grown larger, the stakes in companies have increased, and the funding environment has become more competitive, general partners need a team to help them succeed. This is exciting because it brings more diversity of thought and perspective to a firm, but also because it means the pathways into venture capital are proliferating. Regardless of your role in a firm, however, it's important to understand how everything rolls up into the ultimate goal, which is legally defined as a **fiduciary duty**. In other words, because you are managing other people's capital, you have a legal obligation to act in their best financial interests.

The team at a venture capital fund usually falls into three categories: the investment team, the operations team, and the platform or portfolio services team.

The **investment team** is led (in order of seniority) by the general partners, who then hire principals and associates to help them source, select, and add value to their investments.

- *General partners*, or GPs, typically split their time fundraising, sourcing, selecting, and adding value. As part of their investment terms, many general partners will take **board seats** at companies in which the fund has invested, called **portfolio companies**. Joining the board means they have legal voting and governance rights in the company, a closer pulse on its day-to-day operations, and the ability to exact influence over the company's key strategic and tactical decisions. Depending on how many board seats a general partner takes, and where they are located, this can be a very time-consuming but highly significant part of their role.

- *Principals* are general partners in training. They are not yet owners in the firm, but they share many of the responsibilities. Typically, they focus on sourcing new investments and conducting diligence during the selection process.

- *Associates* are tasked with supporting principals and general partners, which usually means helping source new deals as well as do deeper analysis and quantitative work during the selection process. This often includes building revenue models, collecting financial information, and reaching out to references.

The **operations team** makes sure that the firm functions efficiently and in a regulation-compliant manner. These roles are administrative in function but highly strategic to the long-term success of each fund. They focus primarily on the process of making and managing investments, and they include but are not limited to:

- *Legal* teams that are often brought in-house to help the firm efficiently manage the paperwork necessary for fund formation and finalizing investments.

- *Finance* roles that manage the cash flow, tax, and audit functions of a firm.

- *Executive administrative* roles that are designed to optimize the time of the investment team. Many general partners refer to executive assistants—also known as EAs—as the lifeblood of their firms. They are the people who manage schedules, events, and offices to ensure that all the trains are running on time.

Platform or portfolio services teams are a relatively new part of venture capital firms, but they have become extremely common as the funding environment has grown more competitive and firms have to demonstrate explicitly to founders that they have the ability to add value after they have invested. Usually these teams split their time between managing their function for the firm itself and for the firm's portfolio companies as a value-added service.

- *Marketing* professionals help build the firm's brand, communication, and public relations. They spearhead new funding announcements and serve as a highly valuable resource for portfolio companies that are trying to navigate their relationship with the media.

- *Community* roles are designed to help foster connections within the firm's ecosystem, including portfolio companies, investors, and advisors. They help connect portfolio company CEOs with others at a similar stage or industry, as well as external advisors or firm stakeholders that could be valuable to their company's long-term growth.

- *Talent* teams help both the firm and portfolio companies with hiring and people strategy, and many serve as executive recruiters for difficult-to-find hires that ultimately have a huge impact on the trajectory of a business.

- *Business development* teams are less common but still essential as they are designed to help portfolio companies reach customers in highly strategic or creative ways. Especially when venture capital firms have limited partners that have some sort of strategic value beyond capital (such as corporations or famous individuals), the business development team fosters connections that can lead to revenue.

———

Venture capital is a long and confusing game. It's often difficult to tell what inning you're in, whether or not you're winning, or even who you're competing against. Let me be your coach as we continue on through the nine principles of venture capital investing, along with true stories and provocative questions to help you get in the game, stay in the game, and play to your strengths. If you read on, you will find out how the industry *actually works*, how and why your mindset is more important than your math skills, and what you need to do to demonstrate that you're on your way to the money, power, and influence that you have always dreamed about. There has never been a more exciting time to forge your own pathway into venture capital. Let's get started!

BREAKING
INTO
VENTURE

PART ONE

ACCESS

In the months and years leading up to my journey into venture capital, I was working at General Assembly, a buzzy new education technology startup backed by several well-known venture capital investors. From my very first day on the job as a product manager, when I was one of only a handful of employees, I would wake up in my New York City apartment, roll over to grab my phone from the nightstand, shove my glasses on, and immediately start scrolling through an inbox full of urgent emails.

Potential customers wanted questions answered before making the decision to buy one of our products. Existing customers were encountering challenges with software and needed immediate help or else they wanted refunds. Teammates needed financial information to close out the monthly books before the quarterly board meeting with our investors. Everything was top priority, and I would regularly stay up past midnight clearing my messages, only to wake up a few hours later to a fully replenished inbox.

Instead of thinking of new ideas about how we could build a bigger, better, and more efficient business, I felt like I was constantly struggling to keep my head above water, and it only grew harder the bigger and faster we scaled. When I asked my manager if it might be okay to slow down, I was told our investors were the only ones who could make that decision. Since our investors intended for us to grow our revenues 30 percent quarter after quarter—a condition they set to continue funding the business—we had no choice but to maintain our breakneck pace of expansion. It was clear to me that the people with the money held the power, and I wanted to be one of those people.

Several years later, when I found myself on the other side of the table as an investor at Fresco Capital, I was thrilled to finally be in the driver's seat. I assumed that having money would mean I also had the upper hand, and my primary job would be to sift through the endless opportunities to figure out which companies I wanted to bestow with the gift of my capital. Finally, I was the one with the yes-or-no answer.

After my partner and I set up our new website, I created a new email address, and we raised several million dollars to invest, I didn't know if I should be excited, relieved, or concerned when my inbox was remarkably empty. When I changed my LinkedIn profile from "Regional Director at General Assembly" to "Investor at Fresco Capital," I got a few InMail messages about new farming businesses, a new cancer drug under development, and an "exciting" new idea for importing foreign wine to Hong Kong—none of which were technology companies, nor were they even remotely relevant to what I was looking to invest in, which was primarily software and technology startups solving problems in education and the future of work. Where were the promising businesses fighting for my time and asking me for money? Why wasn't my inbox already teeming with quickly growing startups that were sure to change the world? Wasn't giving people money supposed to be easier than this?

Meanwhile, everyone else I met in venture capital seemed to have no problem finding companies to invest in. They were all getting lucky left and right! We'd meet for coffee, and they'd immediately ask, "So, where do you get your deal flow?" I would try to hide my wide-eyed stare by taking a sip of my drink, while I quietly wondered, *Oh shit, what's that?*

I soon figured out that **deal flow** is your pipeline of new investment opportunities. Deal flow is that line of companies waiting at your door asking you for money (or in my case, not). In an industry where you can make millions on any one successful investment, deal flow is the lotto game you're playing. Except, unlike the lottery, you can't just go to your closest gas station to buy a ticket. You must construct the entire game yourself, and the winners are not randomly announced on the evening news.

According to the Global Entrepreneurship Monitor, 1.35 million tech startups are created globally every year, but fewer than 100 companies per year reach $1 billion valuations.[1] If I was going to make my own luck, I had to make sure I had **access** to those 100 companies every year.

In the early days of venture capital, deal flow was as easy as setting up shop in the right location, and that location was usually Sand Hill Road. Just like fashion has Fifth Avenue, finance has Wall Street, theater has Broadway, and cinema has Hollywood, Sand Hill Road has historically been the mecca of venture capital. As chronicled in Randall Stross's 2000 book, *eBoys: The True Story of the Six Tall Men Who Backed eBay, Webvan, and Other Billion-Dollar Start-Ups*, startup founders used to find their investors by merely driving up and down Sand Hill Road. According to Stross, "The venture guys were seated at the center of the New Economy . . . [they] were the gatekeepers to the world of high-tech startups."[2] If the VCs weren't interested, the startup didn't get funded.

Since that time, the dynamic has changed significantly as technology has served as a powerful force in unseating gate-keepers in all industries—from media to venture capital. The advent of cloud computing drastically reduced the initial infra-structure costs of starting an internet business. Website builders like WordPress and Squarespace meant you didn't need to hire an expensive developer to build your presence. Digital adver-tising allowed new companies to reach potential customers for less money than ever before. No longer throttled by "the venture guys" on Sand Hill Road, the number of new businesses started each year spiked significantly.

On top of that, new forms of funding helped breathe life into thousands of new innovations that may have previously fallen through the cracks. Loosened regulations around the Jumpstart Our Business Startups (JOBS) Act in 2012 and new crowd-funding sites like Kickstarter and GoFundMe made it possible for entrepreneurs to raise startup capital from their personal networks. Accelerator programs like Y Combinator and 500 Startups offered early funding in exchange for equity, and then provided a standardized education program and network of mentors and investors to help promising entrepreneurs build their businesses faster.

As a result of all these factors, the amount of venture capital flowing into startups has exploded since the days of the "eBoys." In 2021, venture capitalists invested $330 billion into technology startups.[3] That's nearly 30 times as much as in 1997, the year eBay was funded.[4] Although this trend has made venture capital infinitely easier to break into, it has also made it infinitely more difficult to navigate; finding great investment opportunities can feel like mining for diamonds in the wilderness. Even if you do find yourself meeting with a company that has world-changing potential, there are likely many other investors who see a similar opportunity. The best companies have a lot of options for where to raise money, and they have the ability to choose who they want to work with.

Getting access to great investments means not only getting the opportunity to meet promising entrepreneurs but also convincing them why they should accept *your* investment when they have a lot of different options for raising money. With millions of new businesses created every year, but only a few hundred reaching the scale they need to be deemed a success in venture capital, you need to build a strategy for reliably attracting the most relevant investments, as well as convincing them they should take your money. Because generating proprietary, relevant, and promising deal flow is foundational to your success in venture capital, the first three principles discussed in this part of the book focus on tools, behaviors, and best practices to ensure you get access to the people, ideas, and companies that increase your chances of building a winning network and portfolio.

PRINCIPLE 1   How You Invest Your Time Is Just as Important as How You Invest Your Money

PRINCIPLE 2   Network Trumps Knowledge

PRINCIPLE 3   Your Investment Thesis Is Your Foundation for Success

---

HOW YOU INVEST YOUR TIME IS JUST AS IMPORTANT AS HOW YOU INVEST YOUR MONEY

Growing up, I watched my parents frequently fight about money. Specifically, that there was not enough of it. As they struggled with technology disrupting their jobs and shouldered the usual burdens of a dual-income household, they worked hard to teach me how to earn and save money. I supplemented my allowance with a variety of hourly jobs and new businesses of my own. I found my very first job when I was in first grade. Our neighbors owned and operated an antique shop. They would go away for several weeks at a time to procure antiques and needed someone to feed their cat, Candy. They offered me one dollar per day. I was eager for the earnings, which felt like a fortune to me at that time. The only catch was that their home was naturally filled with very old things, which I assumed must

9

be haunted. Every day, it took me hours to muster up the courage to walk down the block and enter their historic home, but possibly encountering ghosts was worth it to me for that one dollar.

I steadily increased my potential for earning money once I was legally allowed to obtain gainful employment at the age of 15. I earned eight dollars per hour at my first job at the café within a Lifetime Fitness, where I was tasked with making smoothies, assembling sandwiches, and preventing young children from stealing the energy bars on display (the third task was by far the most challenging). I was always hustling to make more money, so it was not intuitive that money is not actually the most valuable asset in the world—*time is*.

Did you know that the US government physically prints 73.6 million $100 bills every month?[1] That is equivalent to $7.36 billion that appear out of thin air every 30 days, or $245 million every day. Contrast that with an hour of your time; you cannot replicate, extend, transfer, or hold it. When you give or sell an hour of your time, whether for one buck or eight, that hour is inherently irreplaceable and irreplicable. But you don't have to wait for the Feds to produce more of it; time is readily available.

To start thinking and acting like a venture capitalist, you don't need to have a huge pool of money to start writing checks into startups. In fact, you will earn better returns if you focus first on investing your time. That means:

1. Invest time in places where there is a high concentration of what you are looking for.

2. Invest time in building relationships with high-quality connectors.

3. Invest time in ideas that get you out of bed in the morning.

Following these steps will help you best use, protect, and scale your time as an investor, which is the first critical component in ensuring you are accessing the right opportunities.

STEP 1

INVEST TIME IN PLACES WHERE THERE IS A HIGH CONCENTRATION OF WHAT YOU ARE LOOKING FOR

One night, a policeman is doing his typical evening neighborhood walk. The sun has set, and he's on high alert for any potential danger as he strolls slowly down the street. Soon, he comes across a professionally dressed man frantically pacing beneath a streetlight, periodically dropping to his knees to look between the cracks of the sidewalk. He is desperately offering $100 to any passerby who can help him find his misplaced keys. Relieved at the sight of law enforcement, he asks for the policeman's help and explains that he urgently needs to get home to his family. Together, they search every inch of the sidewalk, the gutter, and the road beneath the light and come up empty. Anyone they have enlisted for help similarly gives up after finding nothing beneath the streetlight.

Frustrated and disappointed, the policeman finally asks, "Well, sir, are you sure you lost them here? Is there anywhere else they could be?"

The man replies, "Well, no, I actually lost them in the park across the street, but the light is better over here."

This tale encapsulates a concept commonly known as the streetlight effect. Its origins can be traced back to a Turkish parable from the thirteenth century, but the concept has been repeated throughout history in everything from jokes about people who lost their keys to scientific explanations of observer bias in which observers only see what they expect to see. The point is that you can spend a lot of time searching for something, but if you're looking in the wrong places, you'll never find it.

Unfortunately, in my early days of venture capital, nobody told me this story, so I immediately started searching for deal flow where it was easiest: in Hong Kong. I had a strong personal network and brand

in the Hong Kong region, and I had no trouble finding local entrepreneurs who wanted to pitch Fresco Capital for funding. I spent my
days meeting with new companies that were willing to come to my
favorite coffee shop on Hollywood Road in Hong Kong, though they
were not the businesses I was most excited about or thought were
most likely to go on to be massively successful. Soon, I found myself
with an extremely packed schedule but little excitement about any
prospective investments. At the end of every week, I would sit back
and wonder where the time went. I was growing self-conscious that I
had nothing to show for my packed schedule.

> You can spend a lot of time searching for
> something, but if you're looking in the
> wrong places, you'll never find it.

I had been investing my time in meeting with local entrepreneurs, a strategy that wasn't producing results. Clearly there was a
light shining directly in front of me in Hong Kong, but I had a feeling
my keys were across the street in a park somewhere. I knew I had
to stop doing what was easy and start looking beyond Hong Kong
for deal flow. Along with my business partner, I began to spend my
time researching the major hubs of entrepreneurial and tech activity
that had a high concentration of entrepreneurs seeking funding. I
also hunted for those who had produced big outcomes in the past
decade (unlike Hong Kong, which was still early in its journey as a
startup ecosystem and did not have as many examples of successful
venture-backed businesses). Then I hit the road.

My partner and I spent time in cities like San Francisco, Austin,
and New York, as well as London, Beijing, and Singapore. I spent
the better part of my first five years in venture capital on a plane
(mostly in middle seats in economy, to be exact). On each trip, I was
energized by the entrepreneurial buzz in each region we visited and
overwhelmed by the number of promising companies we met in each

place. My days were equally jam-packed, if not more so, than my time at home. However, unlike my experience in Hong Kong, each day of meetings was yielding exciting investment opportunities that I was eager to dig into. Time flew by, and I was finally producing results. I had real deal flow! I just had to get on a plane to go get it.

As a new, small fund, we were on a shoestring budget, so I crashed on friends' couches or stayed in inexpensive Airbnbs while I was traveling. Especially when it came to navigating the San Francisco Bay Area, I could not have felt more like an outsider. Who knew that Google's headquarters in Mountain View were at least an hour from downtown San Francisco, and that distance ballooned into several hours during rush hour, which in California started not at 5 p.m. like a person might usually expect, but instead at 3 or 4 p.m.? One trip, in hopes of cutting down on travel times, I picked the halfway point between my meetings and splurged on a budget motel in Daly City. I arrived, suitcase in hand, only to discover that the hotel was located directly across the street from a junkyard filled exclusively with old school desks, and that Daly City was affectionately referred to by locals as "Daly Shitty."

It certainly wasn't exactly what I had originally envisioned happening once I was on the other side of the investing table, but it was fun and energizing to be hunting for opportunities, trying to find the diamond in the rough or the next big thing. We were simultaneously in the process of raising our fund, so when we did make an investment, it was a very small amount. We were, however, investing a lot of our time in developing new sources of deal flow. This meant we were gaining access to new investment opportunities in the near term, but we were also building a network that would yield opportunities in the long term. We were building relationships, and we were also gathering experiences along our journey that would serve as data points for calculating how investing our time in certain relationships, activities, and concepts was impacting our fund returns. This feedback loop was essential for further refining and developing our time investment strategies going forward.

Immediately after each trip, I would complete a "travel summary" where I logged how many companies I met, how many were viable investment candidates, and how many I ended up investing in. Later, I could add in what outcomes resulted from each of these companies. I called this process calculating my **deal flow ROI**. How were my time investments paying off in terms of access? This type of rigorous analysis helped me figure out if I was truly investing my time looking in the right places.

Sarah Smith, a partner at Bain Capital Ventures with whom I've shared ideas, drinks, and coffee over the years, holds a similar philosophy. When I asked her opinion on the key to success in venture capital, she pointed out, "It ultimately comes down to where you are spending your time to gain access to new investment opportunities. Of the companies you have met, how many ended up raising successful rounds of funding? That is a good proxy to see if you are swimming in the right pond." This practice—tracking what percentage of companies you have met go on to raise successful rounds of fundings—is standard at most large venture funds. In fact, they systematically track funding announcements and index exactly what percentage of the funded companies they have met.

Indexing every single announcement with that level of precision requires significant resources, but it is easy to simply take the time to check in with yourself on a regular basis. How many of the companies you met in the last year ended up raising successful rounds of venture funding? If the number is fewer than 25 percent, you may need to adjust your sourcing strategies and expand the pool of potential investments you have access to.

STEP 2

INVEST TIME BUILDING RELATIONSHIPS WITH HIGH-QUALITY CONNECTORS

What I consistently found through my time investment analysis was that the best investment opportunities were introduced to me by high-quality people—what I call **connectors**, or people who are highly incentivized (or simply enjoy) introducing investors and startups. Even today, after building a strong foundation of inbound deal flow that yields thousands of potential investments per year, I invest a lot of my time in continuing to cultivate relationships with high-quality connectors. I'll cover a few key categories of common types of connectors here, but remember that high-quality sources of deal flow can come in any shape or form, so stay on the lookout!

Directors of Accelerator Programs

Accelerator programs invest a small amount of money in exchange for equity in startups and are therefore incentivized to help the startups grow bigger and faster. The success of these programs is measured by what percentage of their graduating startups get funded. More funded startups mean the program is more effective and the value of its investments go up. Therefore, program directors are eager to put their companies in touch with investors who may participate in follow-on rounds of funding following your initial investment.

Spending your time accessing these folks makes sense because they have their finger on the pulse of which companies are gaining momentum and which ones aren't; they can confidently point you in the right direction so you don't waste your time with companies that sound great but objectively might not be doing well.

Angel Investors or Seed/Pre-seed Funds

Although it may seem counterintuitive to spend time sourcing deals from other investors, there is a lot of power in building relationships with investors that focus on similar types of companies but don't have the exact same investment strategy. Perhaps these other funds lead investment rounds and you are more of a coinvestor, or they invest at a slightly different point in a company's life cycle. Maybe they simply have different strengths and ways of adding value than you do. No one investor can provide *everything* a company may need to succeed, as each is limited by their strategy, scope, lived experience, and check size. Finding collaborative funds that complement your approach is a great way to access high-quality businesses.

When a company is still an idea on a piece of paper, a founder will usually raise money from friends and family, angel investors in their network, or pre-seed or seed funds that focus on providing funding before the product or business actually exists. These investors work very closely with a founder to make their idea reality and then find additional funding to continue to grow the business. Spending your time with these types of very early investors can help you get to know the DNA of a company you might invest in, and they are also motivated to connect you to their investments because it ensures that those companies will survive and increase their value over time by raising additional capital, also known as a follow-on round.

Regardless of what stage you are investing in yourself, getting to know these earliest investors is an excellent way to access deals through the people who have been there from the beginning and therefore usually know the company best.

While getting to know investors from the earliest days of a company's life is helpful, so is spending time with the investors who are likely to continue funding businesses after you do. Typically, after a company has raised enough capital to get their product off the ground, they search for **product-market fit (PMF)**, or concrete evidence that customers want what they are selling and are willing to pay for it in a predictable way. Finding this inflection point allows founders to quickly shift their focus from figuring out what works to growing what works.

While the name, size, exact stage, and definition of investment rounds have changed over time (the exact parameters of pre-seed, seed, Series A, Series B, and Series C rounds, and so on have evolved and continue to evolve in real time), there remains an important distinction between funds that focus on investing in companies that are pre-PMF (known as **early stage funds**) and those that focus on investing in post-PMF growth (known as **later stage funds**). Later stage funds look to develop relationships with companies over the course of several years before they invest. This is because once a company finds PMF, it is significantly de-risked and there are many more investors who are willing to put money in, which means it can be much more competitive to gain access to the opportunity to invest. Therefore, later stage investors will spend years investing their time to gain credibility with founders, well before they are asked (or get) the opportunity to invest.

No matter what exact round of funding you are focused on, and no matter what exact round of funding these later stage investors are focused on, it is strategically advantageous for them to make high-value introductions to earlier stage investors who are willing to fund the business until it reaches an appropriate size for them to consider. Investing time with these funds that invest in rounds after you is valuable because they will introduce you to companies they have identified as promising and are eager to invest additional capital into later on—if the companies are able to hit certain milestones that indicate they are ready for scale.

Service Providers

Startups need services beyond just investors. They need bankers, lawyers, accountants, and other service providers to help them operate effectively. Many of these service providers seek to build relationships with companies early on, before they are big, with the expectation that if the company grows to be a big, successful business one day, it will end up being a very large client for their firm. A famous example is Amazon Web Services (AWS), a provider of cloud hosting for websites and businesses, which took on Airbnb as an early customer at drastically reduced fees. As Airbnb grew into a billion-dollar business, they ended up paying AWS millions of dollars per year in hosting fees. Because of stories like this, AWS and other service providers have long-term sales strategies to service very early stage startups, even if they have to offer the startups lower fees or flexible payment plans. In a way, they are taking a bet on the long-term success of their clients, and the more funding their clients raise, the more likely their bet is to pay off. Investing time with smart lawyers, bankers, accountants, and service providers who know firsthand if a company is doing well or not, and also want to see that company raise capital from investors, is a great way of generating high-quality deal flow.

Portfolio Founders

If you have already invested in a founder, or you already know and trust them, they are a great source of introductions to other high-quality founders. Similar to how scouting works in sports, you have to have a deep knowledge of the game to spot who is likely to be the next superstar. In most cases, founders love making introductions to investors simply because they experienced fundraising themselves and enjoy the process of making it a little bit easier for others experiencing the same challenges. They also may see making introductions as a way of investing in a relationship with you, as an investor. You never know when they might need to ask for money next!

It was a founder who initially introduced me to Jomayra Herrera, who at the time we met was an investor at the Emerson Collective, an investment firm established by Laurene Powell Jobs, who was married to Silicon Valley legend Steve Jobs, cofounder and longtime CEO of Apple. A Florida native, Jomayra was the first person in her family to go in college, and I had a tremendous amount of respect for how she had successfully broken into venture capital. I immediately connected with her thoughtful, no-bullshit approach to making investments. We shared a similar desire and commitment to investing in building authentic relationships first and figuring out their business value later. As a result, we have spent a lot of time collaborating over the years. She was one of the first people I called when I decided to write this book because I knew she was living the principles I wanted to share.

As we caught up over Zoom on a gloomy San Francisco morning, Jomayra emphasized that venture capital is not just about investing money, but it's about building trust with high-quality people, including your own team, coinvestors like me, and founders you know are going to be successful. For example, she knew from the very beginning that she wanted to build a relationship with Ruben Harris, the founder of Career Karma. During her early days as an investor at Emerson Collective, she made a seed investment in the company based on her thesis around the explosion of college alternatives and the need for guidance and accountability for career development platforms in technology.

"I was one of the first institutional investors, and since then, I have spent years building trust with Ruben," she shared. "I helped him raise his Series A and Series B, spent nights and weekends reviewing materials and making introductions, reviewing candidates, doing whatever I could to make him successful. I invested a lot of time in the relationship."

During her time at Emerson Collective, Jomayra was economically incentivized to do whatever she could to make Ruben successful, because the firm owned equity in the business and Jomayra's compensation was tied to the success of that investment. However, when Jomayra left Emerson Collective to join a different investment fund, she gave up her "carry," the compensation tied directly to Career Karma's success. At that point, she technically no longer shared the same incentives as Ruben, but she knew her relationship with Ruben was still one she wanted to continue to invest her time in.

"These types of trusted relationships: you can't build them with the mindset that you will get something out of it, but if it's the right relationship, you definitely will," Jomayra told me. "Founders are the ones who will speak about you when you're not in the room. If you show up for them, they will speak about you in a way that will inspire others to want to work with you or take capital from you. Ruben has made countless introductions to entrepreneurs I have invested in since. He has served as a reference for me when I am working to close a competitive investment." Jomayra's investment in the relationship is still paying off today, just not in the way she had expected.

The No Asshole Rule

Besides understanding incentives and calculating a deal flow ROI after several interactions with a new relationship, there is also a certain X factor when it comes to finding long-term partners in your journey of gaining access to the best possible investments in venture capital. This X factor can be as simple as the person not being an asshole. I've had plenty of meetings with potential coinvestors or collaborators who started the meeting by sitting back in their chairs and asking, "So . . . who are you again and what do you want?" Or who answer a call from their friend in the middle of our meeting. My favorite has always been those who drop a lot of names of famous people they know (usually I don't recognize them) and offer to make connections but never respond to an email again.

Emergence Capital is a multibillion-dollar venture capital fund known for its pioneer investments in business-focused software (also known as enterprise software as a service, or enterprise SaaS) before this segment was widely considered to be an obvious bet. Although it's not necessarily a household name, Emergence is legendary among aspiring venture capitalists for making only a few investments per year and generating some of the best returns in the industry. They are also famous for their early investment in something that *is* a household name for most Americans: Zoom. Because his firm's reputation precedes him, I was excited to interview Joe Floyd, a general partner at Emergence Capital, for this book. Joe and I immediately connected over our time spent in Asia before permanently relocating to San Francisco, and his own experience as an author of graphic novel *Silicon Heroes* about the unsung heroism of entrepreneurship.

After spending time working in banking and exploring his roots in Asia, Joe found his way to venture capital more than a decade ago. When he started out his career investing at Emergence Capital, he asked his more senior partners, "What do I have to do to be a great venture capitalist?" He was told, "All you have to do is two things—one, follow through on your commitments, and two, don't be an asshole. If you do that, you'll be in the top 10 percent of the greats." Which brings me to an important point. Even if a connector seems "high-quality" at first, it is not worth your time investing with assholes.

Buried in the minefield of personalities in technology and venture capital, however, there are gems: people who approach your conversations with curiosity; people who really listen to what you are looking for and offer to help; people who are willing to be equally open with what they are looking for; people who teach you something new by sharing their latest interests; and people who leave you feeling more energized than you were before. These relationships—the ones that generate momentum—are the ones to treasure, nurture, and invest your time with. You may not know where they will lead or how they will pay dividends in the long run, but they will be worth it.

STEP 3

INVEST TIME IN IDEAS THAT GET YOU OUT OF BED IN THE MORNING

In venture capital, your job is to invest in new businesses, people, and ideas. Because so many of these innovative concepts are extremely improbable (battery-powered cars, a computer in your pocket, a social network where your content disappears!), it is fair to say that both curiosity and optimism are prerequisites for the job. As a curious person myself, I can attest that almost anything is superficially interesting to me, which makes it very difficult to determine where to invest my time. However, there is a clear distinction between the ideas that are intellectually interesting and those that fire up all your neurons and get you out of the bed in the morning.

After more than half a decade of heavily investing my time in building relationships that would serve as access points for great investments, I had finally built a powerful engine for referrals. I was meeting dozens of promising companies per week, but I was still unsure of myself and insecure about being "good enough." Did I have enough deal flow? Was I looking in the right places? After spending years focused specifically on the future of work and technology transforming traditional industries, I worried that my thinking was too narrow. Shouldn't I be looking at *everything* if I wanted to hit it big? So I decided to open up the floodgates and start looking at all sectors, ranging from cybersecurity to deep technology infrastructure to consumer goods and e-commerce.

Although many of these companies had built beautiful products and were posting impressive growth numbers, I found myself procrastinating to avoid digging deeper on the details. The businesses checked all the boxes of high potential investments, but I didn't feel any spark. Instead, what intrigued me most was still the future of work, the technology unlocking barriers to entry for new careers, the companies building products to make teams more collaborative and efficient, and the payment platforms for hiring international contractors. Before I made any investments, I knew I wanted to be spending time on these ideas and with the people solving these problems.

Especially once you have a signal that you are passionate about a particular idea, market, or concept, investing time in understanding the key players in the landscape is one of the best investments you can make. Many great investors spend weeks, months, or years learning about a sector or a landscape before deploying a dollar of capital. How big is the market? How is it segmented (what are the companies and business types within that market)? Who are the dominant players, and where do they fall short? What are the buying patterns of customers? Many investors refer to this process as **market mapping**, and it is an important prerequisite for making good investments. Although market mapping, when done correctly, can be a time-consuming, ongoing research project, having an in-depth understanding of the market shines a bright light on areas of potential profit.

Vanessa Larco is an investor at one of the oldest and largest venture capital firms in the United States, New Enterprise Associates (NEA). Originally hailing from Miami, Vanessa spent years as an entrepreneur and then as a product leader at venture capital–backed companies like Twilio and Box. When she first got into venture capital, she focused on meeting as many companies as possible but quickly realized that she needed a better way of qualifying where she should be spending her time. "There just weren't enough hours in a day," she told me. She soon discovered the secret to prioritizing opportunities. "You have to fall in love with an idea. You have to obsess over it on the weekend and spend a ton of personal time digging into every detail you can. Then, you know you're on the right track."

> Once you have a signal that you are passionate about a particular idea, market, or concept, investing time in understanding the key players in the landscape is one of the best time investments you can make.

For Vanessa, it was women's reproductive health that she found herself thinking about nonstop. In her early days as an investor, she spent over two years understanding the key stakeholders, incentives, and technologies in the space, ranging from menstrual health, contraception, and fertility to postpartum care and menopause. She invested hundreds of hours meeting companies leveraging technology to build better solutions for treating women before meeting one particular founder who Vanessa believed had the right product, evidence of sales momentum, and a killer team. "I fell in love," she recalled, "but getting access to invest in the company was only possible because I had invested so much of my time in market mapping first." By investing her time first, she was able to demonstrate to the founder that she had a unique knowledge of the market, she was aligned with their mission, and she was likely to be able to add more value than other investors who had not done the same amount of work up front.

Investing time in researching a market before making an investment paid dividends for Joe Floyd as well. In his first few years at Emergence Capital, he was drawn to the concept of video collaboration tools and soon found himself spending a lot of time researching the idea that we were on the cusp of a replacement cycle for old video technology like Webex and Citrix that was now falling woefully short of what newer technology had made possible in his personal life.

"We were digging deep into one company as a potential investment, and as part of our due diligence process, we were trying out all the competitors. We wanted to make sure we knew the whole landscape, and we were heavily investing our time ahead of our capital. My partner was in Argentina and had a terrible cell connection, so we tried Zoom," Joe told me on a phone call.

When Zoom worked infinitely better than any other solution the team had tried, Joe's partners at the firm reached out directly to the founder of Zoom, Eric Yuan, to propose making an equity investment in the company. Emergence Capital ultimately made billions on the investment, but it was only possible because of the time investment they made in following an idea about new video collaboration software first.

In venture capital, like many other industries, it takes years to create an overnight success. Whether or not you have a venture capital fund or a job title that includes the word *investor*, you can start building toward that success by investing your time wisely. It may not always lead where you expect, but that's half the fun!

BREAKTHROUGH TIPS
FOR INVESTING YOUR TIME WISELY

- Start by taking stock of your time investments as you are making them. Consider taking a week to log the people, places, and ideas you currently spend time on, for how long, and what results it generates.

- Identify where there is a high concentration of what you are looking for. Don't be afraid to get on a plane and go there. Video connections are useful, but being present in person is powerful for generating momentum.

- Set a cadence quarterly where you measure your deal flow ROI—how many companies have you met, and how did you connect with them? Who are the high-quality connectors who have opened doors that led you to interesting companies that you have considered for investment? These are the people you should be investing more time with.

- Focus not just on results but also on your gut instincts about people. Good connections you make should be opening doors, giving you energy, and generating momentum. No assholes allowed.

- Identify three to five top ideas that get you excited and spend at least 15 minutes per day learning more about them in some way.

- Be patient with time investments; they can take years to pay off, and they often yield unexpected returns.

NETWORKS TRUMP KNOWLEDGE

Whenever I teach a course on venture capital, without fail, the most popular question from my students is, "What is the mathematical process of valuing a startup? How do you apply the right multiple to their revenue numbers to arrive at a proper valuation?" No matter how many equations, case studies, or scenarios we run, however, my students are never satisfied with the answer. What I have tried to emphasize, but nobody wants to hear, is that your valuation methodology is essentially irrelevant when it comes to creating your own success in venture capital.

You can optimally value a startup and write a technically airtight term sheet (whatever that means), but if you don't know the right people to make it possible to actually complete an investment in your target companies, your skills are completely useless. *People* create access, and access is the primary essential ingredient for successful venture investing. This is the cold hard truth: it's not *what* you know that will allow you break into venture capital; it's *who* you know.

Nasir Qadree is the founder and sole general partner at Zeal Capital Partners, a $60 million venture capital fund backed by blue-chip financial firms like PayPal, BB&T, and SunTrust. Nasir and his team focus on backing diverse management teams building businesses that turbocharge economic mobility. This includes technology solutions improving educational outcomes, promoting financial wellness, and helping individuals find better jobs. As Nasir and I have crossed paths over the years at conferences, looking at the same investments and raising capital from the same limited partners, it has been obvious that we share similar values and opinions about the power of venture capital as an industry for change. However, it wasn't until I invited him to guest lecture in my course at Columbia Business School that I realized how his own story of breaking into venture capital could serve as a powerful guide for students who still believed that cap table math and perfect term sheet construction held the keys to their future.

As we connected to formally dive into his origin story for the context of this book, we had to work hard not to drift off topic given how much we always have to talk about. Once we finished debriefing on the beautiful and meaningful art in his perfectly curated Zoom background, he shared that early in his career, he never planned to build his own venture capital fund, nor did he think about how he could break into the industry. Instead, in search of financial independence, he started his career on Wall Street. Eager to feed his passion for entrepreneurship and social justice without compromising his reliable salary, he kept his full-time job and as a hobby, teamed up with a few of his friends to open a coffee shop in the West Village in 2011. They called it the Bee's Knees Baking Company and set up shop in the heart of New York University's campus, a location that serendipitously placed them on a direct collision course with the budding entrepreneurs spending their days running between classes.

As a naturally curious and effortlessly charismatic person with an instinct for making connections, Nasir loved getting to know his customers and asking what they were up to and what he could do to be helpful. He soon noticed that many of them were spending their time in the shop meeting with venture capitalists, and their number one priority as entrepreneurs was meeting more potential investors in their companies. It was clear that if Nasir wanted to be helpful, he should get to know more venture capitalists. Although his only personal financial investment at that time was the coffee shop itself, his curiosity about the world of investing in startups was piqued. Who were the people funding these new tech companies? He started to learn more about the businesses his customers were building as well as the types of people who were funding them.

As his knowledge grew, so did his interest in applying his financial skills to the world of entrepreneurship. Filled with questions about how to do that, he soon found himself gravitating toward spending time with other investors who started to let him in on their way of thinking by sharing the basic ins and outs of venture capital, opening up their network of potential deals, and connecting him to other active investors. He was hooked. "What can I say, I have a knack for building a strong social Rolodex," Nasir recalled, "and I knew I was on the cusp of something that was going to open doors to even more interesting people and ideas."

It was that growing social Rolodex, along with his ability to navigate it effectively, that ultimately helped Nasir land a highly sought-after role at Washington D.C.–based venture firm Village Capital as their global head of education investments. Although he had to pass up an equally sought-after spot at Yale Business School to accept the job, Nasir has never looked back. "There is no cookie-cutter way to break into venture capital, especially as an African American investor. It would have been nice to say I went to Yale, but fast-forward to where I am today; I didn't get here because of business school, I got here because of the folks I met along the way."

Nasir's humility is certainly part of his charm, but what he's leaving out is that he is a master in turning chance encounters into meaningful relationships, mapping those relationships into a powerful personal network, and navigating that network to accomplish his goals. Whether you're looking to break into a new industry, find your next job, meet your future partner, or learn about a new concept, accessing great opportunities requires converting friendly acquaintances into powerful allies. In venture capital specifically, gaining access to great investments requires cross-referencing the right people across multiple networks at once, including limited partners, founder/CEOs, and other venture capitalists.

> Whether you're looking to break into a new industry, find your next job, meet your future partner, or learn about a new concept, accessing great opportunities requires converting friendly acquaintances into powerful allies.

This process of building and leveraging a personal network is a complex yet critical skill that is not taught in classrooms, but in this chapter, I'll guide you through how to meet high-quality connectors in six simple steps:

1. Write your own narrative.

2. Focus on the people you already know.

3. Make it easy for people to help you.

4. Consider the quality of your introduction.

5. Remember the back channel.

6. Make sure your reputation precedes you.

These critical steps will help you build a powerful platform of collaborators in the categories discussed in Principle 1—high-quality connectors like directors of accelerator programs, funds with strategies that complement yours, service providers, and other founders. These people will ultimately form your network, which is the vital source of your proprietary deal flow, one of the most important foundational pieces of success in venture capital.

STEP 1

WRITE YOUR OWN NARRATIVE

I have thousands of business meetings every year, and they all pretty much start the same way, whether they are with founders, coinvestors, collaborators, potential investors, or anyone else. On my way to the meeting, I type the other person's name into LinkedIn or search my email to try to understand the context and purpose for our connection. As we sit down or log into Zoom, we look at each other and silently wonder, *Who are you, really, and what can you do for me?* but figure out how not to ask the question too directly since it can be jarring. Of course, some people come straight out and say, "Why are we meeting?" but most have the social tact to at least start with pleasantries that may provide clues as to why we are investing this time with each other. This may seem odd to those who don't spend the majority of their days building their network, but in venture capital, it can be far too easy to lose track of who you're connecting with and why.

Regardless of your opening banter, the person sitting across from you needs to know who you are and what you are looking for if they are going to provide value to you, and it's largely up to you to define that for them. Otherwise, they'll construct a story about you on their own, and it will likely not be nearly as powerful as what you can write yourself. Even if they do the work to look you up online in advance, your LinkedIn profile will never adequately convey what makes you special, what makes you worth listening to, and what makes you worth helping.

Chip and Dan Heath, in their bestselling book *Made to Stick: Why Some Ideas Die While Others Survive*, provide a useful framework for how to convert simple ideas into unforgettable stories. The framework they provide applies to personal narratives as well. The introductions that last beyond a single conversation are:

- **SIMPLE.** Because we know everything there is to know about our own lives and backgrounds, it can be tempting to get into all the nitty-gritty details about how things happened. Being memorable requires finding the core of your own story: what is the one central idea, problem, or experience that drives you? Avoid complexity and embrace the singular, central, most important thing about you.

- **UNEXPECTED.** Getting and keeping attention requires an element of surprise. Home in on what might be unusual and unique about you, your background, and/or your experience. How do you break the mold? What about you may be different from how you first appear?

- **CONCRETE.** Help people understand and remember you by providing specifics about where you have been or what you have accomplished. How many users did you scale your company to? How much money did you raise? Don't be abstract, be tangible.

- **CREDIBLE.** Make sure your story is believable. It certainly needs to be true, but you can reinforce its accuracy by providing convincing details or providing external validation to corroborate what you've said. Sharing credentials, awards, or common connections helps validate your authority as a storyteller.

Whether you're speaking to an investor you're hoping to bring in as a limited partner, another venture capitalist you'd like to refer deal flow to you, or a founder you're hoping to invest in, having a strong personal story will make sure they remember you and tell others about you too. Many students find it surprising that I teach the art of the personal narrative in my venture capital classes. Especially for those who aspire to be investors, it can seem awkward to need to have a compelling personal story.

We typically start with an exercise where everyone writes out their answers to the following questions:

- Where are you from?

- Why are you here?

- What is something about you that may be surprising?

- What is your proudest accomplishment?

- What are you trying to do next?

- What do you have to offer?

Although not easy to write down at first, pulling from these answers can yield powerful introductions like that of Jomayra Herrera, a general partner at Reach Capital, where she invests in education technology startups. She has always been passionate about education because, as mentioned in Principle 1, she was the first person in her family to go to college. She graduated from Stanford with a bachelor's degree in political science and a master's degree in education policy. After spending time working at BloomBoard in customer success, she has spent the last eight years investing in education technology companies. She sits on the boards of several billion-dollar companies and is frequently featured in *TechCrunch* and other leading publications about her expertise in education policy, company building, and investing.

Jomayra's background is *simple* (education is a key theme for her), *unexpected* (it is unusual for an education investor to be the first college graduate in her family), *concrete* (we know where she grew up, what companies she invests in, and where her work is featured in the media), and *credible* (her credentials include leading universities and well-known publications). As another venture capitalist focused on this space, I am immediately compelled to reach out to Jomayra with new investment opportunities because I know she had a unique expertise, point of view, and ability to add value to the business if we were to work together.

Or take Danielle Strachman, cofounder and general partner at 1517 Fund. Danielle founded and ran a charter school in San Diego, California, and after witnessing firsthand the shortcomings of the education system in America, she joined Peter Thiel (the billionaire founder of PayPal) to establish his Thiel Fellowship program. The program was specifically designed to enable entrepreneurs to be successful without taking traditional educational pathways, and they provided $100,000 grants and a network of support for founders willing to drop out of college to build a company instead. After backing dropouts who started multibillion-dollar businesses like Vitalik Buterin, the founder of cryptocurrency Ethereum, and Dylan Field, the cofounder of Figma, Danielle and her cofounder established a venture capital fund dedicated to investing in startups run by teams without college degrees.

Danielle's narrative is *simple* (focused on college dropouts), *unexpected* (most people don't go from starting schools to starting venture capital funds), *concrete* (I know who she has worked with in the past), and *credible* (she has clearly had success already). I know exactly what Danielle is looking for, what she can do for people, and why others would be compelled to work with her. It's no wonder we've become close collaborators and good friends over the years.

Your narrative can change over time and can change according to your audience. The good news is you get to write each iteration; the bad news is you get to write each iteration. Controlling the narrative to your personal story is empowering because it puts you in the driver's seat when it comes to creating a lasting (and accurate) impression on your audience. It is also challenging because you can't blame anyone else if your narrative doesn't land. Start by writing it down by hand and testing it out on a few new connections. Just remember the framework from *Made to Stick*: keep it simple, unexpected, concrete, and credible.[1]

STEP 2

FOCUS ON THE PEOPLE YOU ALREADY KNOW

My first day as a venture capitalist, a tropical storm was pouring sheets of cold rain across the entire city of Hong Kong. I was based in Central Hong Kong, but I had agreed to meet my new partner, Tytus closer to where he lived, on the campus of City University of Hong Kong, which was about an hour's train ride. I bundled up in my best rain gear, which was fashionable but horribly unsatisfactory for the intense horizontal rain. I still remember looking at myself in the mirror before heading out into the storm. My army green rain jacket cinched at the waist and my long hair peeking out from beneath my hood, I wondered if I looked like an investor as I had hoped, or if I still looked like the startup entrepreneur and community organizer I had previously been. It didn't matter, I told myself. I was going to be a venture capitalist now, no matter what my outfit said.

When I showed up to the office, I had no idea what to expect. Without a strong network of professional venture capitalists myself, I had never stopped to ask, "What exactly do you do all day?" I suppose I assumed our primary focus would be evaluating companies to invest in. After all, my partner was a well-known and prolific angel investor, and the classes he had taught at General Assembly on angel investing were largely focused on how to access and analyze great investments. This is precisely why I was so surprised when the first thing he said to me when I arrived was that our first order of business was going to be raising a new fund. I mistakenly assumed he had that part figured out already! I understood that **accessing**, **analyzing**, and **adding value** were part of the job description, but I had largely ignored the **accumulate funds** part of the equation.

My immediate reaction was total panic. I had no idea how to raise a venture capital fund. I also didn't know anyone who invested in venture capital funds. I was in my mid-twenties with practically no personal savings or family wealth. Where could I possibly start? It was clear that I needed to build a relevant network of investors to help us accumulate funds if we were going to be successful long-term. How could I meet more people like Tytus? I recovered from my initial panic by bringing to mind the process I had used for building my network in Hong Kong that had led me to him in the first place.

When I decided to take the leap to move to Hong Kong from New York, I had quickly adjusted my personal narrative to include that fact, hoping it would lead to new connections I could leverage as the foundation of my network in a new city, country, and continent. Every conversation I had in the months leading up to my departure included the fact that I was moving halfway across the world to Hong Kong to establish a business that educated working professionals in technology and entrepreneurship, just like the one I had just helped build in New York. I was looking to meet anyone in Hong Kong who worked with startups. It was *simple* (one sentence only), *unexpected* (I was a white woman from the Midwest living in New York with no existing ties to Asia), *concrete* (I made it immediately clear what I needed), and *credible* (I had established this type of business before).

After constructing this narrative, I had started with the people I already knew. I spoke to my colleagues at the time, and one of them had a friend from college who had grown up in Hong Kong. He lived in Boston then but served as an important reference for learning the basics about this new territory. My roommate in New York City had an ex-boyfriend from high school, Paul, who then lived in Hong Kong and was an entrepreneur. Despite all the years and distance, they were still on good terms, and she put us in touch. Paul was one of the first people I met in Hong Kong, and he quickly introduced me to Jason, another friend of his who was a web developer and might be interested in teaching a class. After Jason and I met for coffee, he had introduced me to two other people: another web developer and the angel investor named Tytus who was now my new partner at Fresco Capital.

Clearly, what had worked was leveraging my personal narrative with my existing network. Once again, I took pen to paper and wrote my new personal narrative and created a list of who I knew already that could be relevant to my new mission of accumulating capital for a new venture capital fund. I then grouped these people into categories and what their primary motivation might be for investing in a fund:

- Successful entrepreneurs who taught classes at General Assembly and were therefore interested in helping other entrepreneurs

- Finance professionals with extra capital and an interest in getting closer to the exciting world of technology and startups

- Government entities that had budgets dedicated to spur innovation in the local economy

- Foundations or nonprofits committed to education or entrepreneurship

- Angel investing networking groups who might want a more efficient way of connecting with startups

Beneath each category, I listed people's names. I was surprised that I had more ground to stand on than I had originally thought, 15 or 20 people to start. I reached out to each one with a simple email request for advice. After all, as Pitbull emphasized in his song "Feel This Moment" featuring Christina Aguilera, if you ask for money, you will likely end up with some useless advice. If you ask for advice, however, you may just end up with some money.

Here is a sample of the email I sent:

Subject: Update and advice?

Hi Olaf,

Hope you are well! It was such a pleasure working together on your recent class about transitioning from a career in finance to starting your own business. It was a hit with the students, and I hope you enjoyed it as much as I did.

As you may have heard, I recently left General Assembly for the world of startup investing. I am now setting out to raise our first venture capital fund focused on education and the future of work.

As someone I respect who is well connected in the world of finance and entrepreneurship, I'd love your advice on the process. I'd also love to see if there are ways we can continue to collaborate!

Are you free for a coffee sometime next week?

Best,
Allison

I used contact management software to log each and every one of my meetings, taking note of each person's reaction to my personal narrative, whether or not they were interested in the opportunity to invest themselves, and any introductions they offered. I also made sure that I spent time during the meeting asking what they were working on and what mattered most to them at that moment. This would allow me to provide value in return. At the end of every day, I followed up with a note thanking them for their time, offering anything I could to help them meet their goals at the time, sharing information about our new fund, and requesting introductions to the specific individuals they mentioned.

From there, my network grew, and I was enlisting each member of my network in my ultimate success. I also built trust by making it clear I was invested in their success as well. By following this process through hundreds and hundreds of meetings, Tytus and I raised several million dollars, and we were ready to start investing. As I turned my time and attention toward gaining access to great investments, I began applying this same methodology to generating deal flow. *Who did I already know that might be a high-quality connector in the category of directors of accelerator programs, investors with strategies complementary to mine, service providers, or startup founders? Or, even if I don't know one of these people directly, who might be able to introduce me?* All I had to do was adjust my personal narrative to resonate with my new mission of meeting startups. Following is a sample of one of the emails I sent.

Subject: Connecting to seed stage companies?

Hi James,

Hope you are well! It was such a pleasure getting to work with you as an instructor for our Web Development course last year at General Assembly. As you may have heard, I recently left General Assembly for the world of startup investing and am now running a small fund dedicated to investing in companies transforming education and the future of work

As someone I respect who is well connected in the world of technology and entrepreneurship, I'd love your advice on any founders, companies, or other investors in your network I should be spending time with.

I'll be in New York next week. Are you free for a coffee? Let me know some times that work best for you, and I'd be happy to meet wherever is most convenient. Of course, I'd also love to hear what's new with you and explore other ways we can continue to collaborate in my new role!

Best,
Allison

As a result of my email, James and I met for coffee, where he told me he happened to be looking for a new role and was in the middle of meeting quite a few early stage companies during his interview process. He offered to connect me to several that seemed promising, and before I knew it, I had several more meetings lined up within a matter of days. James was interested in my opinion on the companies he was interviewing as well, as he only wanted to work for a company that was likely to be well funded in the future. Taking the time to listen to what matters to others can often result in mutually beneficial connections.

STEP 3

MAKE IT EASY FOR PEOPLE TO HELP YOU

Whether you are focusing on people you already know or cultivating new relationships, developing a strong personal narrative and learning about what matters to the person sitting across the table from you are key components in building trust and *motivating* other people to *want* to help you. However, no matter how well-intentioned your contact may be, they are also constantly struggling to allocate their most valuable resource—their time. Following up quickly after you meet (within 24 hours or less) and making it as easy as possible for the other person to take action on your request for help are both essential elements for ensuring you get what you are looking for. Here's an example:

Subject: Great to see you!

James,

It was great to see you for coffee this morning. Thank you again for taking the time! It's very exciting to hear about your new role as CTO at Smithson & Co! You mentioned you are looking for office space in Midtown. If it is helpful, I'd love to introduce you to my friend Alice Wong, who runs a coworking space in the area. Let me know and I would be happy to put you in touch.

You mentioned I should connect with Kyle Daniels, the Director of the FastTrack accelerator program in New York. Below is a blurb about me if helpful for making an introduction. I'm in town the rest of the week and would love to meet him while I am here.

Hi Kyle,

I'd love to introduce you to an old colleague of mine, Allison Baum, who is now an investor at Fresco

Capital. Their fund invests in seed stage companies focused on the future of work, and she was interested in meeting you and some of the companies going through your accelerator. She was also an early employee at General Assembly and would be happy to share her learnings from building and scaling a venture-backed EdTech startup if helpful! Would you be open to a connection?

Best,
James

Thanks again and look forward to our next coffee!

Best,
Allison

A version of this email helped me make several high-quality investments within several weeks of my meeting with James. Here's why:

- I followed up quickly on our meeting, within 24 hours: *It was great to see you for coffee this morning!*

- I recognized that his time is valuable: *Thank you for taking the time!*

- I demonstrated that I was listening and that I care about what matters to him: *It's very exciting to hear about your new role as CTO at Smithson & Co! You mentioned you are looking for office space in Midtown.*

- By offering him something in return that I know he is looking for, I created additional incentive for James to reply: *If it is helpful, I'd love to introduce you to my friend Alice, who runs a coworking space in the area.*

- I reminded him of the connections he offered to make *and* provided a quick and easy way for him to reach out on my behalf. Now, instead of needing to compose a new email, James can simply copy and paste my blurb to Kyle: *You mentioned I should connect with Kyle Daniels, the Director of the FastTrack accelerator program in New York. Below is a blurb about me if helpful for making an introduction.*

- I created a sense of urgency to make the introduction now instead of waiting until later: *I'm in town the rest of the week and would love to meet him while I am here.*

Over the years, I have used this same email format to follow up on time I have invested with all different stakeholders. It has served as a powerful tool to build relationships that lead to accumulating capital from limited partners, as well as accessing great investment opportunities. It also applies for anyone looking to break into the industry or get a job in venture capital. I know this because I also often find myself on the receiving end of emails like this.

As someone dedicated to creating new pathways into the industry, a professor teaching about how venture capital works, and a human interested in paying it forward for all the time others invested in me over the years, I reserve several hours per month to meet with individuals referred through my network who are looking for advice on how to work in venture capital. There is a wide variation in the follow-ups I receive after my meetings, but I always respond to requests that take the format of the second example below. Otherwise, it's far too easy to get distracted by other priorities. For example, I often receive emails like this:

Subject: Nice to meet you

Hi Allison,

Great meeting you yesterday. I'd love to be connected to anyone in the SemperVirens HR Advisor network. I'd also love to meet any other investors you think would be a fit for our round.
  Let me know, thanks.

Lauren

If I want to be helpful to Lauren, I now need to spend time thinking about who would be helpful to connect her to. Once I've arrived on people that specifically may be willing to connect with her, I need to compose an entirely new email that explains how we met, who she is, what her company does, and why they should meet. If too much time passes, I may not even remember some of these details. If I do remember, I try to be diligent about including hyperlinks to company websites and LinkedIn pages in my introductions so that the recipient can quickly and efficiently evaluate if they'd like to accept the introduction. That's a lot of work for me to do, and even if I have the best of intentions, there are too many steps where other priorities are likely to take precedent.

Now, consider this email instead:

Subject: Thank you again for your time!

Dear Professor Gates,

It was great to connect you with you this morning, and thank you for sharing your advice on breaking into the venture capital industry. Congratulations on the launch of your newest fund! I know you mentioned you are particularly interested in the idea of enabling remote and distributed work, and a good friend of mine recently left her job at Google to start a company building software to help companies automate the process of vetting international contractors. I'd love to introduce you if you are interested.

You mentioned that I should connect with your friend Jomayra Herrera, whose firm is looking to hire an associate in the near future. Based on what you told me about their focus on education technology, I believe I'd be a great fit for the role. I am interviewing with a few other firms this month, but I'd love the chance to meet with her in the next few weeks if she is open to it!

Below is a forwardable blurb you can share to see if she would be willing to meet. I have also attached my résumé to this email.

Hi Jomayra,

I'd love to introduce you to a student from my most recent course on venture capital who is interested in learning more about the role on your team. Angelina is completing her MBA at Columbia Business School and is interested in learning more about your role. During her time at business school, she built and launched her own education startup focused on helping unemployed teachers find remote work during the pandemic. She is originally from Estonia and also leveraged her network to start a virtual Speaker Series inviting Eastern European startup founders to speak to students on campus, including the founders of Skype and Pipedrive. Let me know if you'd be open to meeting her!

Sincerely,
Allison

Thanks again for your time, and I look forward to keeping in touch!

Best,
Angelina

These types of emails not only make it easy for your connection to help you, but they also demonstrate that you already understand how the industry works and are therefore far more likely to succeed within it. In a simple interaction, you have shown that:

- You are investing your time ahead of your capital.

- You understand how to get **access** to the introductions and opportunities you want.

- You can **analyze** a situation and identify what matters to key stakeholders.

- You are able to **add value** to the person you are interacting with.

- You know how to maximize your odds of getting the outcome you want.

STEP 4

CONSIDER THE QUALITY OF YOUR INTRODUCTION

In each of the preceding examples, I've discussed how to leverage who you know to access the opportunities you are looking for. When it comes to making the most out of your network, it's important to consider not only *how* you ask for an introduction, but also *who* you ask for an introduction. In many cases, if you are looking to get in touch with a specific investment firm or a specific company that you are interested in investing in, a simple request for an introduction may not always result in a connection. Making it easy for someone to reach out on your behalf is only half the battle; the other variable is how well that person knows the person they are offering to introduce you to.

In a world where time is scarce, people tend to prefer taking referrals from sources they know well and trust. For example, I ignore all **blind introductions**. Blind introductions are when someone reaches out to connect me to somebody else *without asking me first*. This is a common tactic for people who like to identify as **super-connectors**, or people who measure the quality of their network simply by how many people they have in their contact list. They are often very quick to offer a connection but will not take the time to check on both sides if there is mutual interest, a process called **opting in** to a connection.

Opting in to introductions allows people to filter out opportunities without any clear ROI or relevance to their current goals. Successful founders and venture capital investors receive hundreds, if not thousands of emails, phone calls, messages, and social media pings a week. How do they decide which ones to respond to and which ones to ignore? Much of that decision depends on the reputation of the person offering to connect you—are they a high-quality connector? Are they trusted by their network? How well do they know the person they're reaching out to on your behalf? Before asking for an introduction, do your homework to ensure that you're following the right pathway into the opportunity or person you're hoping to access.

IS THIS PERSON THE RIGHT PATHWAY FOR AN INTRODUCTION?

If you're looking for a way to get introduced to an investor, an entrepreneur, or a potential job opportunity, you may be able to see on LinkedIn if you have any contacts in common. Or perhaps someone within your network has already offered to connect you. In an ideal world, there may even be multiple pathways you can leverage to meet your desired connection.

What are the criteria you should use to determine whether or not to ask a mutual connection for an introduction? Your connector is considered high quality if they have *at least* one of the following three key criteria:

1. The connector knows you well and can vouch for your abilities related to whatever reason you are requesting the introduction. For example, you are looking for a job at a venture capital firm and you ask your former boss, who thinks very highly of you, to reach out to make a connection to the general partner there.

2. The connector knows your desired contact very well and is trusted by them. It's very difficult to refuse an introduction from someone whose opinion you value. For example, you are looking to meet an entrepreneur and you are requesting an introduction from an existing investor in their business.

3. The connector has made introductions to this desired contact in the past, and they have proved to be fruitful. There is nothing more powerful than a track record of success. For example, you are looking to meet another investor and you are requesting an introduction through a founder they have invested in previously.

After years of trading introductions, I was excited to sit down with a friend and frequent coinvestor, Kyle Lui, to break down the science behind which introductions he gets and which introductions he gives. Before joining Bling Capital, where he invests in seed stage companies, Kyle spent nearly a decade investing at DCM Ventures, a global venture capital fund with over $4 billion in assets under management and offices in Silicon Valley, China, and Japan. The team at DCM has generated more than 30x returns on their 2014 vintage fund, equating to $10 billion in returns for their employees and investors,[2] a clear indicator that they've finely tuned not only how they invest their time but also their capital.

When it comes to getting access to great investments, it can sometimes be very difficult to get in touch with founders who are building companies that are highly likely to be successful. Especially when there are already plenty of investors interested in putting capital into their business, finding the right pathway to an introduction is the only way to get their attention. As Kyle put it, "In other asset classes, when you decide if an investment is good, you can invest. In venture capital, identifying a good investment is just one part of getting access to it. You also need to win them over, and doing that is all about people and relationships."

Reflecting on how he's been able to build the right relationships with founders that resulted in the opportunity to invest, Kyle identified two key factors: (1) getting an introduction based on common values, or (2) getting an introduction based on a common contact who can vouch for you.

Introductions Based on Common Values, Experiences, and Communities

When Kyle was just getting started, one of the first deals he sourced at DCM was Shift, a marketplace for buying and selling used cars. The company was growing quickly, and the founder, George Arison, was difficult to get in touch with. Over the years, however, Kyle has invested a lot of time in supporting fellow LGBTQ+ founders and investors who have historically been a minority community in the technology and investment industries. As it turns out, George shared a similar mission.

One evening, Kyle and George found themselves seated next to each other at an LGBTQ+ entrepreneurs/investors dinner. They ended up hitting it off, and George was happy to include Kyle on the list of potential investors in their next round of funding, not only because they connected on a personal and professional level, but also because they clearly shared the same values of supporting minority communities in their industries. Kyle knew he wouldn't have gotten access to Shift's investment round if he hadn't discovered that he and George shared a set of common values.

Introductions Based on a Strong Common Contact Who Can Vouch for You

Kyle recalled being very interested in investing in a company called Amber Group, a technology-enabled financial services firm for the crypto industry. Word on the street was they were in the process of completing a very competitive and oversubscribed investment round, but Kyle realized he had worked with one of the company's existing investors before. He called up his contact and asked if he would be willing to introduce him to the founder of Amber Group. A referral from his existing investor, whom he knew well and trusted and who vouched for Kyle and the team at DCM, was enough for the founder to open the door.

"After weeks of trying to get in touch, I was able to get on the phone with the CEO within 24 hours," Kyle recalled. "In the end, we were able to get an allocation in the round after he cut several other firms out of the opportunity." Amber Group is now valued at $3 billion,[3] and Kyle was only able to gain access because he found the right connection who knew both him and the founder well.

Before asking for an introduction, consider how well you know the person connecting you. Also consider how well they know the person you're asking to connect to. Finding the right pathway may take time, but investing in ensuring you're maximizing your odds of connecting is well worth it.

STEP 5

REMEMBER THE BACK CHANNEL

Getting the right introduction is often only the first step in getting access to great opportunities. Of course, someone has to be willing to meet you in order to consider the possibility of working together. But on top of that, they also have to *choose* you.

When I first started in venture capital, I thought making an investment was as simple as saying yes or no. However, in fact, there is a complex decision-making process on both sides—that of the company that is choosing their investors and that of the fund that is choosing their investments. There are often a multitude of stakeholders involved on both sides, and your personal network is a valuable tool in navigating that process and making sure the ultimate decision ends up the way you would like it to. Leveraging who you know to influence a particular situation or outcome is known as the process of **back-channeling**, and it is one of the least discussed but most important components to success in venture capital.

When living and working in Tokyo, I learned about a concept called 空気を読む (*kuuki o yomu*), which is directly translated as "reading the air." Reading the air requires sensing and anticipating the forces at play that are often invisible to the eye. The term is commonly used in business as a way of conveying the importance of knowing the unwritten rules of how things get done in Japanese corporate culture. Although I didn't always like it, I quickly learned that if I was going to get what I wanted, I needed to learn to look beyond the obvious. Who is the *real* decision-maker? What do they want? What are they afraid of? Who are the people influencing their evaluation of this decision? What other factors might be playing a role in the outcome? Although the Japanese phrase is far more poetic than the term *back-channeling*, the same concept of learning the unwritten, invisible, informal networks, practices, and centers of influence applies in Silicon Valley as well.

A critical skill in venture capital is uncovering the power dynamics lingering beneath the surface of any given decision. Determining who the real influencers are is not always as clear-cut as it seems. On the Interaction Institute for Social Change website, Kelly Bates and colleagues explain, "In every organization, there are people who hold formal power and informal power. Formal power is attributed to someone by virtue of their title or position in the organization. People carry informal power if they have influence over others or their organization, either because of their experience, force of personality or persuasion, unearned privilege, or because they have strong relationships with decision-makers and peers."[4]

Whether you realize it or not, an existing network, system, or power structure is conspiring to create momentum toward a certain outcome. In other words, one or more people are pulling the strings behind the scenes. It's up to you to identify what those dynamics are and who you know that might be able to help you. Whether you are looking to get a job at a venture capital fund, or maybe you're already working there and you are trying to evaluate whether or not you'd like to invest in a company, or you've already decided to invest and now you're trying to influence the entrepreneur to say yes, try to figure out who else is involved in a decision getting made. This can be as simple as asking, "What is your decision-making process?" or it can involve reaching out to others who have been through a similar process and can share the unwritten rules they learned on the other side. Then, look for common connections you can enlist in reiterating your message that you are the right person for the job. These common contacts are your **back-channel influencers**, and they are a very powerful tool for getting any kind of deal done.

For example, I was recently evaluating an investment in a company I will call Company V, which credentials and trains healthcare providers in how to work with patients from underrepresented groups. Several days before I needed to make a final decision about the investment, I got a text message from another investor that I have known for several years and is now a well-known and respected expert in mental health and healthcare equity. She told me that she had heard I was looking at investing in Company V and that she was, in fact, an angel investor in the company. Her text message was simple and short, expressing that she couldn't be more impressed and excited about the trajectory of the business. She offered to share her experience working with the founder, as well as get on a phone call to share information she had uncovered during her diligence process. I took her up on her offer and got the opportunity to leverage her expertise in the field, as well as her personal knowledge of the business and the founder, to make my decision. I also asked her to put in a good word with the founder, who was in the process of deciding who he would select as an investor in this funding round. Thanks to this back-channeling, we made the offer to invest, and it was accepted by the founder.

Another investor I've worked closely with over the years, a fun collaborator and a reliable back channel for influencing entrepreneurs and potential limited partners, is Sarah Smith. As I mentioned in Principle 1, Sarah is a partner at Bain Capital Ventures. She was an early employee at Facebook, where she was first introduced to the concept of venture capital because Facebook itself was funded by venture capital investors. As part of her compensation package, she was awarded a small amount of equity in the business, and the idea of sharing in the upside of the company she was building was exciting to her. What she didn't realize was how much more equity was owned by the investors, who were largely behind the scenes until the weeks and months leading up to the initial public offering (IPO). During that time, the major investors who were part of the board of directors had a regular presence on campus, and she couldn't help but notice that they were all men. Curious as to why, she quickly learned it was because all the venture capital funds that backed Facebook in its early days were run by men. Although alarming, it was not unusual given fewer than 5 percent of venture capital investors at that time were women.

It wasn't just the gender divide that shocked Sarah, though. It was the fact that as a hardworking employee building the business day after day, she had significantly less skin in the game than the investors who had funded the company in its early days. "These guys made thousands of times more money off the IPO than I did through my equity as an early employee, even though I was working crazy hours to help the company grow day in and day out. I figured, I can be pissed at those guys, or I can figure out how to *be* one of those guys." She ultimately chose the latter and went on to become a partner at Bain Capital Ventures.

Once she was on the other side of the table, Sarah learned that the process of gaining access to an investment is far more complex than meets the eye because there are unseen players involved. In her journey from startup employee to influential venture capitalist, she learned that although the process of seeking investment and venture capital funds falls on the founder, the CEO of a new business doesn't always have the final say in who can actually invest in their company—the board of directors, which consists of the largest and most influential shareholders, have the final say. Learning to read the air means figuring out who are these other large investors that may control access to investing in a particular business.

In Sarah's early days as an investor, she found herself in a competitive process to lead an investment in a well-known and popular company building software for offices. Whenever a company raises a funding round, there is typically only one **lead investor**, who sets the terms of the investment and typically takes a seat on the board of directors. All the other **coinvestors** put in smaller amounts at the same terms as the lead investor.

"I had known the founder for more than a decade, and I was so excited to invest in his company, which was doing very well at the time, so I gave him a term sheet at a very high valuation. We negotiated and I even upped my offer by 50 percent," she recounted. "He had another offer that valued the company at an even higher number, but he verbally accepted my terms because we knew each other well, and he wanted to work with me personally." She was thrilled. Her years of investing in this relationship had finally paid off in the form of access to a high-quality, and highly sought-after, investment. However, after a few days went by and she didn't hear from him, Sarah got concerned.

The founder eventually called and told Sarah that he had a major problem. Another prominent, well-known Silicon Valley venture capitalist, let's call him Bill, sat on the company's board. What Sarah discovered later was that Bill held a grudge against her firm after a negative experience during his time as an entrepreneur himself. He insisted that the firm had a terrible track record of acting poorly and did everything in his power to convince the founder not to accept Sarah's investment proposal. The founder emphasized that he really wanted to work with Sarah and that he valued their deep relationship and trust more than the other offer at a higher valuation, but he was unable to achieve the outcome he wanted. Bill threatened to sue the founder if he accepted Sarah's term sheet, asserting that not accepting the offer at the highest valuation was a breach of **fiduciary duty**, or the legal obligation to act in the best interest of one's shareholders. Regardless of whether or not this case would have had legal merit, the company and the rest of the board were forced to listen to Bill's opinion.

> The face of the company is not necessarily the final decision-maker, especially if you have particularly loud or influential voices around the table.

Unable to match the other offer, Sarah began back-channeling to try to influence Bill to back down from his aggressive stance. Seemingly still in shock many years later, she recalled in horror, "Bill called me personally and started yelling at me nonstop asking me, 'Who do you think you are offering these kind of terms?!'" The founder ultimately couldn't overcome Bill's aggressive stance and accepted the term sheet from the lead investor with the highest valuation. Sarah's biggest takeaway? "It is important to not only think about founders when you are giving them term sheets, but to do the work to understand who else is on the board and what their motivations are. Talk to the board members and build relationships with them as well, and then you can sell the whole package. Most new VCs don't realize that the current board has a lot of say in the decisions that get made."

Although it was not the smoothest educational pathway, Sarah learned how to read the air very quickly, as this experience made it clear that there are informal power dynamics behind the scenes that ultimately determine which way an investment decision can go.

The face of the company is not necessarily the final decision-maker, especially if you have particularly loud or influential voices around the table. Back-channeling at the last minute is often too late. Invest the time in reading the room, investigating how decision gets made, and building relationships with people who know how the pieces fit together and have the ability to influence the outcome in your favor.

MAKE SURE YOUR REPUTATION PRECEDES YOU

Although it's tempting to believe that you can always identify and reach these **back-channel influencers** who will impact the decisions that can make or break your future, back-channeling often happens without your knowledge. That is why building a reputation that precedes you is the most powerful back channel there is. Every interaction you have with founders, coinvestors, limited partners, and other stakeholders ultimately plays a role in how interested people will be in working with you. You can write the most compelling personal narrative possible, but your reputation is what people say about you when you're not in the room. Invest the time in building a reputation that serves you well, even when you don't know it.

In fact, how you treat people that you *don't* end up investing in or working with is often just as important as how you treat those that you do. Whenever I meet a company and decide not to invest, I make it a point to write them an email stating that we are not going to invest and providing two to three key reasons why not. In many cases, this provides helpful feedback to founders who might not understand how investors are thinking about or evaluating their business. In others, it provides concrete data points that founders can use to follow up with me when their business has progressed to a point where they can provide evidence to answer the outstanding questions I have outlined as the reasons for not choosing to invest.

Similarly, how you treat founders and CEOs at companies that are *not* successful is often just as important as how you treat your massive winners. As Joe Floyd at Emergence Capital aptly points out,

"You make your money on your winners, but you make your reputation on your losers." As he recounted during our interview, Joe learned the power of reputation when he invested in a travel startup that was doing really well until the global pandemic completely decimated their business and their revenue dropped to zero in a matter of three weeks.

> How you treat people that you *don't* end up investing in or working with is often just as important as how you treat those that you do.

Most CEOs make contingency plans for a quarter of slow growth, or losing a few customers, but not for a scenario where they lose all their revenue at the same time. As a result, the company was running out of money, and fast. Joe and the other board members determined that fundraising was not an option, so instead they worked to find an acquirer for the business at a low price. Often called a **soft landing**, these types of acquisitions are designed to save face for all involved. These types of outcomes are not anywhere near the multibillion-dollar returns that founders and investors dream of, but they prevent the company from crashing and burning and declaring bankruptcy. A soft landing generally means that investors might get some of their money back, and the founders and employees still have jobs.

In the case Joe was telling me about, the acquisition price for the company was well below the amount their firm had invested. As a result, the board of directors had the power to decide how much of the purchase price would go to investors and how much would be reserved for founders and employees. Although the initial investment terms dictated that, in this situation, 100 percent of the proceeds should go to investors and the founders and employees should be left with nothing, the investors still had the power to allocate the proceeds as they see fit. To reward the people who had worked hard to get the company to where it was, Joe leveraged his role as a major investor and board director to ensure a **carveout**, which is when investors pro-actively divert some of their returns to the founders and employees.

"We put in a good carveout to make sure the CEO and employ-ees of the company would still earn some return on the time and hard work they had invested, but several angel investors felt they were get-ting shortchanged by the transaction and threatened to sue for breach of fiduciary duty," Joe recalled. "We ended up giving up part of our firm's returns to make sure the deal could go through and the angel investors could still get their money back. The amount of money didn't matter very much to us, but it mattered a lot to the CEO of the company that the deal went through."

Although he gave up some money in the transaction, Joe was investing in something even more valuable—his reputation. Years later, he told me about a time when he was vying for a competitive deal where the founder/CEO was unsure whether to accept a term sheet from Emergence Capital or go with a rival firm. He decided to back-channel his network to find out what it was really like to work with Joe, and he was connected to the CEO of the travel startup Joe had previously worked with to find the soft landing. Although he hadn't talked to Joe in several years, the CEO of the travel startup gave an incredible reference, ultimately convincing the founder to go with Joe's firm as the lead for their investment round. In a world where who you know is more important than what you know, it is impossi-ble to predict the ripple effect of your actions, but you can know with confidence that they will live on far into the future.

BREAKTHROUGH TIPS FOR INVESTING IN GREAT RELATIONSHIPS

- Start with who you know and be specific about your asks. Don't leave people guessing about how they can be helpful—make it clear up front.

- If you have an idea about who you are looking to meet, be strategic about who you ask for an introduction. Does your mutual contact fit the criteria for a high-quality connector?

- Assume that just like you, everyone else is also trying to maximize their time investments. Make it as simple as possible for them to help you.

- Write a personal narrative that is simple, unexpected, concrete, and credible. Don't be afraid to change your narrative based on your audience and your goal—it should evolve over time just as you do!

- Employ active listening to understand what matters to the people you are spending time with and find ways to add value or a way to give back so they can reach their own goals. Win-win may be a cliché, but it's overused for a reason: it works!

- Don't forget to read the air—keep power dynamics in mind. The reality is, you might not know who the people behind the curtain are, so it's important to find out.

YOUR INVESTMENT THESIS IS YOUR FOUNDATION FOR SUCCESS

Getting access to high-quality opportunities in venture capital—both when it comes to jobs and deal flow—requires investing your time wisely and learning to cultivate the right relationships within your network. The next step is understanding how to capitalize upon these relationships to ensure that you are putting yourself in the right position to be one of the "lucky" ones.

As Vanessa Larco pointed out in Principle 1, there are simply not enough hours in the day to meet every single company that has investment potential. Finding a way to efficiently funnel the right opportunities your way—and filter them once they're in front of you—is a surefire way to create your own success without burning out. This requires building a clear and authentic **investment thesis**. It also requires communicating that thesis effectively so you can stay top of mind whenever someone you know and trust is thinking about making an introduction.

As part of this process, every time I meet another venture capitalist, I ask, "What type of investments are you looking for?" This is a powerful mechanism for getting to know another investor, understanding what matters to them, and figuring out if we should invest more time with each other. Does this other person's universe contain a high concentration of what I am looking for? Could they be a high-quality connector? Do they spend time on ideas that get me up in the morning? If the answer is yes, then there is likely to be a high ROI on our time spent together.

During my first few weeks living in San Francisco, I hopped in an Uber to go visit Tina, another VC I met through mutual contacts when I first moved to the Bay Area, at her plush, modern offices in the SoMa district of the city. Tina is a partner at a large, well-known, multibillion-dollar venture fund that invests across all stages, asset classes, and geographies, and the understated luxury of their offices reinforces the impression that they have done very well on their investments over the years. Our mutual contact thought we might have opportunities to collaborate since we share an alma mater and were both interested in supporting other female entrepreneurs. As discussed in Principle 2, a shared community and values often lead to high-quality connections, so I was excited to meet with her. When I sat down on the large leather chair, I asked Tina some variation of my typical question, "What type of investments are you particularly interested in right now?"

Tina replied, "Well, I typically invest in very early stage companies; I'll occasionally invest pre-product. But I also do late-stage growth investments if they are really compelling. I'm interested in B2B [businesses that sell to other businesses] as well as B2C [businesses that sell to consumers], as well as marketplace business models. I'm also actively looking at next generation e-commerce as well as supply chain and cybersecurity. I also have a small pocket of funds that I use to invest in international startups on an opportunistic basis."

I nodded politely, but in my head, all I could think was, *Huh?* As an outsider, I am sure her response sounds like jargon to you, but it was (and still is) just as meaningless to me. She did not share any specifics about who, what, why, when, or where she invests, nor did she provide any coherent narrative to what ties her areas of interest together. As a result, I left that meeting with very little understanding of what Tina was looking for. Instead, my understanding was that *Tina* might not know what she was looking for, either. In the five years since that meeting, I have never sent Tina a single investment opportunity.

By contrast, I always know what to send Jomayra Herrera because she has always been abundantly clear about what she cares about: investing in education and future of work technology that democratizes economic opportunity in the United States. "The reason I got into venture capital was not because I wanted to be an investor; it was because I believed there were opportunities to solve specific issues based on my personal background," Jomayra told me. "Growing up in a low-income household with Puerto Rican parents in a family where no one had attended college, I wanted to work closely with founders leveraging technology to change education and economic mobility in America. Those are the types of investments that have always mattered to me."

Not only is Jomayra specific about what she invests in (education, future of work, increasing access to jobs), but also why (her upbringing), where (in the United States), and when (at the early stage, when she can work closely with founders to build from the ground up). Her clarity of thought has helped her make successful investments in companies like Handshake, a network for individuals seeking entry-level jobs that reached a $3.5 billion valuation. It also helps her network understand what types of companies to refer her way for introductions. Since we first connected over half a decade ago, Jomayra and I have regularly exchanged investment opportunities—too many to count. If a few months go by and we haven't connected, I'll come across one of her regular tweets or her latest blog post outlining what she cares about most right now, and I will be reminded to reach out to get her opinion on an investment opportunity or back-channel to check if she has met with a company I am evaluating.

So how do you avoid following in Tina's footsteps and instead find a path to high-quality introductions like Jomayra? I'll guide you through how to build and leverage an investment thesis in five steps that will help you get access to the right types of investments at the right time, significantly increasing your odds of success.

1. Figure out *why* there is an opportunity. How is the world changing?

2. Define *what* you will invest in—your scope of opportunity by sector, industry, business model, technology, or problem.

3. Identify *when* in a company life cycle you want to invest.

4. Select *where* geographically you will be focused on finding companies.

5. If relevant, define *who* you believe will build the most valuable businesses of the next generation.

Once you have internal clarity on your focus, you will need to communicate your thesis clearly and memorably to attract opportunities your way. Leverage the same tools and framework that you used for your personal narrative. Finally, be aware that you will need to adapt your thesis over time as you gain more information and the world changes. After all, venture capital is an industry investing in the power of change—that means you have to be able to adapt too.

STEP 1

FIGURE OUT *WHY* THERE IS AN OPPORTUNITY. HOW IS THE WORLD CHANGING?

Venture capitalists and technology CEOs love to quote Wayne Gretzky, who may or may not have actually once said, "Skate to where the puck is going, not to where it's been." Whether or not he deserves the attribution, this statement drives home the point that in venture capital, we are investing in the future. A typical venture capital fund lasts *10 years*, and the most successful investments take that long to reach a big enough scale to generate outsized returns (after all, no matter how amazing you are, it takes time to build up to $100 million in revenue per year). Given this time scale, it is very difficult to discern what might be a good investment if you don't have a clear picture on what you believe the future will look like. That is why the first step to building an investment thesis is to identify what the world will look like 10 to 15 years from now and what the key drivers are for that change.

A typical venture capital fund lasts for *10 years*, and the most successful investments take that long to reach a big enough scale to generate outsized returns.

One of the most well-known examples of an eerily accurate future vision statement came from Marc Andreessen, cofounder of Netscape and the multibillion-dollar venture capital firm Andreessen Horowitz, also known as "a16z" for the 16 letters that sit between the *A* in Andreessen and the final *z* in Horowitz. In 2011, Marc outlined his investment thesis in the *Wall Street Journal* under the title "Why Software Is Eating the World."

Not only did his thesis have a catchy title, but he painted a very clear picture of how the world had changed and what he believed the world would look like in another 10 years. He said specifically, "We are in the middle of a dramatic and broad technological and economic shift in which software companies are poised to take over large swathes of the economy. More and more major businesses and industries are being run on software and delivered as online services—from movies to agriculture to national defense. . . . In the next 10 years, I expect at least five billion people worldwide to own smartphones, giving every individual with such a phone access to the full power of the internet, every moment of every day. . . . The result is a global economy that for the first time will be fully digitally wired."

He went on to explain why this was happening then and what the key catalysts were that would propel us into the future he envisioned: "Six decades into the computer revolution, four decades since the invention of the microprocessor, and two decades into the rise of the modern Internet, all of the technology required to transform industries through software finally works and can be widely delivered at global scale."

He went on, "On the back end, software programming tools and Internet-based services make it easy to launch new global software-powered start-ups in many industries—without the need to invest in new infrastructure and train new employees. In 2000 . . . the cost of a basic Internet application was approximately $150,000 a month. Running that same application [in 2011] costs about $1,500 a month."[1]

Marc Andreessen and his cofounder of a16z, Ben Horowitz, were both internet entrepreneurs, having founded Netscape and Loudcloud respectively. Although those names might not mean much today, they were heavyweights of the early days of the internet. This experience gave Marc and Ben front-row seats for the critical changes in consumer behavior, as well as the transformation of back-end infrastructure, that he identified as a key driving change toward the world he envisioned.

Similarly, I drew upon my personal experiences to formulate my investment thesis around investing in the future of work, which I published in 2018.[2] After seeing technology replace traditional jobs like those of my parents and building a business to train individuals in technology skills for new types of jobs, I envisioned a future in which the traditional notion of "employment" was replaced by a more flexible, digitally based, and data-driven mode of work. Why was workplace automation happening now? Between 2000 and 2014, technology served as a catalyst for improving business productivity (that is, the output that businesses ultimately delivered to their customers) by 80 percent, but wages only increased by 1 percent.[3] That meant 30 percent of the workforce,[4] or nearly 50 million people in the United States, need more than one job to make ends meet. That was leading 70 percent of all workers to actively seek new jobs,[5] which was growing increasingly complicated given that new technology such as artificial intelligence would, by some estimates, automate up to 47 percent of existing jobs in the next 10 to 20 years.[6] Finally, a new generation (my generation)—millennials—was just becoming the largest generation in the workforce,[7] and they are imposing their new value system—shaped by the internet, social media, and the Financial Crisis of 2007–2008—on their employers.

The best way to formulate a clear vision for the future is to draw upon your personal experiences. Ask yourself:

- What has been unique about my life that may indicate other people's lives are changing in a similar way?

- What problems have I experienced firsthand that are likely to impact large numbers of people or businesses in the future?

- What skills or strategies have led me to success that can be applied to other companies or industries?

- What changes have I personally witnessed that I believe are likely to continue? What data have I aggregated and synthesized that indicates there is a large shift underway?

STEP 2

DEFINE *WHAT* YOU WILL INVEST IN—YOUR SCOPE OF OPPORTUNITY BY SECTOR, INDUSTRY, BUSINESS MODEL, TECHNOLOGY, OR PROBLEM

Once you define your expectations for how the world will be different in the next 10 to 15 years, you need to make that vision **investable**. To be investable, a scope needs to be *specific, differentiated, and actionable*. In other words, how can you actually make money off the changes you are predicting? It's certainly satisfying to be right, but it's even more satisfying if you've become a world-class venture capital investor as a result!

In "Software Is Eating the World," Andreessen translated his vision into an investable scope of opportunity when he said, "Software is also eating much of the value chain of industries widely viewed as primarily existing in the physical world."[8] He goes on to specifically identify these industries as financial services, cars, retail, healthcare, and financial services. This led the firm to buy valuable stakes in companies in those sectors, like Coinbase (financial services; a cryptocurrency wallet), Flatiron Health (healthcare; health technology company focused on digitizing cancer research), Lyft (cars; ride-sharing), and Dollar Shave Club (retail; e-commerce for razors), each of which resulted in billions of dollars in returns for the firm and its investors.

To be investable, a scope needs to be *specific*, *differentiated*, and *actionable*.

Throughout his time at DCM Ventures, Kyle Lui was able to draw up on the firm's deep roots in Asia to track how economic demographic shifts were accelerating change at different paces in different parts of the world. After witnessing firsthand how technology was impacting certain industries in China or Japan, the team at DCM then used these data points to formulate a vision for what the future in the United States might look like as those same dynamics played out in a different country. During our interview, Kyle described how his colleagues in China had experienced how rapidly growing urban populations in Chinese cities created problems for commuting as massive numbers of people were overstretching an inadequate public transportation infrastructure. This led them to envision a future that included new ways of getting around in cities, an investable opportunity called *micromobility*, a term used to describe the problem of moving large numbers of people or goods over short distances.

After the firm made several wildly successful e-bike and scooter investments in China, Kyle started hunting for an analogue in the United States. "That's when I met Brad and Toby, the founders of Lime, now one of the leading scooter businesses in the country. I knew very quickly there was an opportunity there," he said. In other words, Kyle was able to source an introduction to Lime through his network because he knew what he was looking for, and others did too. Once he connected with them, he identified very quickly that he should invest his time (and soon, his money too). All of this was possible because of his vision of the future of transportation, and his ability to distill that vision into an investable theme of micromobility. It is specific because he provides a tangible example of what micromobility means in the form of bikes or scooters. It is actionable because these types of businesses exist today and are raising capital from venture investors. It is also differentiated because only a small percentage of venture investors are focused on this area.

Here are a few different filters you can apply to arrive at an investable thesis that is specific, actionable, and differentiated:

- **SECTOR OR INDUSTRY.** Many investors explicitly state that they invest only in specific sectors, like healthcare, financial services, agriculture, cybersecurity, advertising, or gaming.

- **BUSINESS MODEL.** This means you focus on a specific mode of making money, the most popular being B2B (businesses selling to other businesses), B2C (businesses selling to individual consumers), or marketplaces (platforms that charge a transaction fee for matching buyers and sellers).

- **TECHNOLOGY.** Focusing on developing technologies. The internet of things (the ability for any object to connect to the internet, not just computers and phones), artificial intelligence, machine learning, cloud services, and quantum computing all fall into this category.

- **PROBLEM.** Large social issues like climate change, economic mobility, an aging population, exploding levels of student debt, or access to healthcare also help define a specific scope of investment focus.

When it comes to my investment in the future of work, I distilled my vision of a digital, distributed, and data-driven economy and a new type of relationship between employers and employees into a specific, actionable, and differentiated scope that includes three sectors and one type of business model: healthcare technology, financial technology, and workforce technology companies that are selling B2B. Why? Employers provide their employees with healthcare, wages, and work. The problem is that what employers provide today across those three categories are inadequate. Employer-sponsored healthcare has only been focused on physical health, leading to an explosion in mental healthcare costs as the American death rate from drugs, alcohol, and mental disorders has nearly tripled since 1980.[9] Employer-provided wages have stagnated, leaving 69 percent of Americans between the ages of 18 and 64 with less than $1,000 in savings.[10] And the jobs themselves suck, with more than 80 percent of workers reporting they are so unhappy at work that it has affected their personal lives.[11]

Sharing this level of specificity led my network to connect me to companies like Spring Health, an employer-sponsored mental healthcare benefit providing millions of employees of companies like Gap, Sysco, and Amazon with access to mental healthcare. Because I knew this type of business fit squarely into my thesis, I immediately started investing time in getting to know the mental health landscape. SemperVirens Venture Capital was able to make an investment in the seed round of Spring Health, when the business had only a few customers. Only a few years later, the company has grown in valuation by over 100 times.

STEP 3

IDENTIFY WHEN IN A COMPANY LIFE CYCLE YOU WANT TO INVEST

Once you distill your future vision of the world into a specific, actionable, and differentiated scope, you must also decide what stage of a company you want to focus on. This is important for two reasons—the first being that further narrowing your scope to include a stage helps protect your time. As I've discussed, millions of businesses are being started every year, and a multibillion-dollar business takes at least 5 to 10 years to build. That means that at any given moment, there are millions and millions of companies to sift through to effectively identify and gain access to great opportunities. Investors like Tina who identify as **stage-agnostic** (investing at any point in a company life cycle) tend to miss out on access to great opportunities because their network doesn't have an efficient way of identifying if something fits into their scope. As I've mentioned, finding focus helps ensure more efficient time investments.

The second reason is that the skill set required for effectively analyzing and adding value to your investments varies dramatically based on the size and stage of those companies. We will spend more time on how to effectively analyze and add value to investments in Parts Two and Three of this book, but in the meantime, identifying what stage fits your knowledge base is also a critical tool for getting access to the right opportunities.

Millions of businesses are being started every year, and a multibillion-dollar business takes at least 5 to 10 years to build.

Venture capital is typically divided into four main stages: pre-seed, seed, early, and growth. Each comes with its own check size, expected returns, risk level, and mindset.

Pre-seed

Investing in a team and an idea before they have any customers or product is the pre-seed stage. If a billion-dollar business is a massive oak tree, and it grows by planting a seed, you are investing in a team that tells you they plan on getting the seeds, but they don't have them yet. You are often investing alongside friends and family.

- **TYPICAL CHECK SIZE.** $10,000 to $100,000

- **TYPICAL VALUATION.** Less than $10 million

- **REVENUE.** 0

- **TIME TO GENERATE RETURNS.** 10+ years

- **RISK LEVEL.** Very high risk of failure (greater than 50 percent) balanced by a high expected return (100x+)

- **MINDSET.** Without any product to try or customers to interview, you are purely betting on people and their ideas about how the world is changing. You love working closely with your investments; you love running experiments and gathering data to figure out what works. You have a lot of trust in entrepreneurs, and you want to be building alongside them.

Seed Stage

Investing in a team, an idea, and a minimum viable product, which is the seed that gets planted and hopefully grows into a large, lucrative oak tree, is the seed stage. Usually companies will have one or two customers or users, proving that there is some demand for their product, but there is still a big question of how much.

- **TYPICAL CHECK SIZE.** $50,000 to $2 million

- **TYPICAL VALUATION.** $5 million to $25 million

- **REVENUE.** 0 to $500,000 per year

- **TIME TO GENERATE RETURNS.** 8 to 10 years

- **RISK LEVEL.** High risk of failure (at least 50 percent) balanced by a high expected return (10x to 100x per company)

- **MINDSET.** You are still betting on people and their ideas about how the world is changing, but you have some initial evidence based on a product and early customers. You like meeting a lot of companies and selecting your investments based on your intuition, not necessarily on data. You are often driven by a motivation to find "the next big thing."

Early Stage

Investing once an idea has turned into a real business that has paying customers but is still only a few years old is the early stage. Early stage investing typically includes Series A and Series B investment rounds, each of which involves selling 20 to 30 percent of the business's equity to help a company reach critical mass for scale. This stage of investing brings less risk than seed investing because there is a real product, business, customer base, and track record from the team to analyze, but it is still early in the company's life cycle. For example, Uber and WeWork were located in only one city when they raised their Series A funding rounds.

- **TYPICAL CHECK SIZE.** $2 million to $10 million

- **TYPICAL VALUATION.** $25 million to $100 million

- **REVENUE.** $1 million to $10 million per year and growing at least 3x annually

- **TIME TO GENERATE RETURNS.** 5 to 8 years

- **RISK LEVEL.** Relatively high risk of failure (about 30 percent) balanced by a high expected return (10x to 30x per company)

- **MINDSET.** You like making big bets, but you prefer to have more data to analyze to ensure you are making informed decisions. You have a specific expertise in how to help companies grow faster and usually have a more institutional/finance-driven mindset.

Growth Stage

Investing in a proven business that can grow faster with additional capital. This usually includes investments rounds from Series C to the initial public offering (IPO). This style of investing is significantly more quantitative and involves analyzing large amounts of data that are available given that there is an established market, mature product, and repeat customer base. Growth rounds require a clear path to exit via a large merger, acquisition, or public offering in the next several years.

- **TYPICAL CHECK SIZE.** $10 million to $100 million

- **TYPICAL VALUATION.** $100 million to $1 billion+

- **REVENUE.** $10 million+ per year and growing 1.5x to 2x annually

- **TIME TO GENERATE RETURNS.** 1 to 5 years

- **RISK LEVEL.** Low risk of total failure (less than 30 percent) with slightly lower expected returns (2x to 3x per company)

- **MINDSET.** You enjoy taking your time to get to know a business, team, and market and prefer to leverage concrete data to make predictions about the future. You are patient, willing to wait a significant amount of time to find the right moment to invest in a company at the right valuation. You enjoy a slower pace of investing, with only one to two investments per year, and are proficient in complex Excel spreadsheets, modeling out various scenarios, and studying the competitive landscape.

Similar to the process of finding a sector, problem, or theme to focus on, finding the right stage for you is a matter of triangulating your personal experience, preferences, and skill set with where you see a particular opportunity in the market. Focusing on a particular stage provides clarity and makes it easier for both you and your network to filter the right opportunities your way. Danielle Strachman at 1517 focuses exclusively on pre-seed and seed stage investments. I've reached out to her with a company I'm interested in many times, and she will decline the introduction because the company is too late stage. She is helping me fine-tune my referrals for her, and she is also protecting her own time by avoiding focusing on companies that do not fit her focus area.

Focusing on a particular stage provides clarity and makes it easier for both you and your network to filter the right opportunities your way.

STEP 4

SELECT *WHERE* GEOGRAPHICALLY YOU WILL BE FOCUSED ON FINDING COMPANIES

Incorporating a location lens into your thesis can serve as a critical building block of your vision of the future. Or, more simply, it can merely serve as a useful filter for protecting and efficiently allocating your time. Although Silicon Valley remains the global headquarters for venture capital, accounting for nearly 40 percent of dollars invested in the United States,[12] we live in an increasingly global, distributed startup ecosystem. Unlike the early 2000s, venture-backed companies in the 2020s hail from all 50 states.[13] So do their investors—the number of active investors located outside main hubs of activity like the Bay Area, New York, and Boston has tripled in the last 10 years.[14] That has created a tremendous amount of opportunity to tap into previously undiscovered categories of entrepreneurs and can also lead to a seemingly unlimited number of potential investments to meet. Getting access to the right ones requires getting narrow enough that you can invest your time wisely.

For example, funds like the Rise of the Rest Seed Fund have an explicitly location-driven thesis. Launched in 2017 by AOL cofounder turned venture capitalist Steve Case, the fund focuses on seed stage investments in high-growth technology companies outside of the coastal tech hubs of New York, Boston, and San Francisco. Disillusioned with rising housing costs in major cities like San Francisco, the team at Rise of the Rest believes that the future of innovation is based in less expensive cities like Orlando, Louisville, Tulsa, and Austin, where entrepreneurs can build businesses with a more efficient cost basis.[15] When I connected with the team there, it was very easy to remember what types of companies to send their way, as well as what types of companies they could provide me with access to—all because they have a specific, differentiated, and actionable geographic thesis.

The same trends apply to the global startup ecosystem. Dedicated regional funds have grown in popularity as non-US markets like India and China have started to produce multibillion-dollar businesses in the last decade. In 2021, Silicon Valley A-lister Sequoia Capital launched their second dedicated seed fund focused exclusively on early startups in India and Southeast Asia. The fund's vision of the future is based on rising smartphone adoption in India, with the expectation that within 5 years, there will be a billion connected users in the country, and within 10 years, India will be producing world-class software businesses they can sell internationally.[16]

Whether it's an international focus, a unique US-based focus, or merely the discipline to say, "We do *not* invest outside of the United States," identifying your geographical focus is an important step in fine-tuning your investment thesis.

STEP 5

IF RELEVANT, DEFINE *WHO* YOU BELIEVE WILL BUILD THE MOST VALUABLE BUSINESSES OF THE NEXT GENERATION

In the last decade, there has been more attention called to the fact that the overwhelming majority of venture dollars have been invested in a very specific type of founders—that is, white males. As the media and the venture capital industry alike have shone a light on why that may be the case, there have been more and more investment theses and funds focused on directing funding to founders and CEOs from underrepresented backgrounds that may have been historically over-looked by the traditional venture capital ecosystem. Female Founders Fund was established in 2014 when only 2 percent of venture capital dollars were going to female-founded companies. Their thesis was based upon the fact that despite their lack of funding, women start businesses at a rate 1.5 times higher than the national average, and companies with female founders on the team perform 63 percent better than companies with only male founders.[17]

Defining your thesis by founder demographics is not a necessity, but it is one of the many ways you can narrow your focus to ensure you are gaining access to the best investment opportunities in a time-efficient manner.

Creating your own luck requires putting yourself in the way of lucky things—that is, creating a system by which relevant and highly qualified opportunities find their way to you. Especially in the early days of building your deal flow pipeline, it can feel awkward to automatically decline introductions or pass on investment opportunities. However, it is precisely your willingness to *not* spend time with the *wrong* companies that will enable you to spend time with the *right* ones. Even if you have the right mindset when it comes to investing your time and you have cultivated a powerful personal network, it is impossible for you to get access to the right opportunities if you don't have a clearly articulated vision of what you are looking for. You can become a magnet for incredible opportunities if you take the time to outline your vision for the future and translate that vision into an investable thesis that incorporates a target sector or opportunity, stage, and geography.

BREAKTHROUGH TIPS FOR BUILDING AN INVESTMENT THESIS

- Dig deep into your personal experiences to create your vision for the future 5, 10, and 15 years from now. Is your vision specific and differentiated?

- What are actionable ways you can invest in your vision? What types of companies are capitalizing on the trends you believe will shape the next decade?

- Be realistic with yourself about your skill set and what stage of investing is the best fit for your network, attitude, interests, and abilities. Where do you have a significant edge in not only accessing, but also analyzing and adding value to investment opportunities?

- Consider realistic constraints on your thesis to ensure that it is actionable. Do you have the right resources, skills, and capital to invest according to the sector, stage, and opportunity set that you have defined?

- Don't be afraid to say no to introductions, even if they seem great on the surface. If they don't fit into your investment thesis, filter them out and respect the time of all those involved.

PART TWO

ANALYZE

What separates a great venture capitalist from a casual investor? As we have learned, the first step is creating a sustainable way of getting access to the best possible investment opportunities. The next step is actually choosing to make good investments. But in a fast-paced world filled with big ideas and endless possibilities, how can you possibly tell the winners from the losers? **Due diligence** (DD) is the process of analyzing each opportunity carefully and ultimately deciding whether or not to invest. Although DD can sometimes seem like a version of the scientific method, it is also a form of art. In this section, you will learn best practices for evaluating investment opportunities, as well as which data points deserve more weight than others. We will also discuss how to build a process that leverages your unique strengths and insights while also accounting for your biases. Additionally included here are ideas on how to evolve that process over time as you gather new information, collect new experiences, and witness new outcomes that will shape and reshape your thinking over time.

No matter where you start out, your destiny is determined by the decisions you make. Both life and venture capital are filled with forks in the road—choices to be made, paths to be taken, and others to be passed by. Sometimes when I'm feeling tired and melancholy (usually when it's raining or I'm sitting in a plane on a tarmac somewhere), I think about all my major life choices and wonder *what if*. What if I had stayed in the States and never moved to Asia? What if I had not called off a wedding in my twenties and started a venture fund instead? What if I had moved from Tokyo to New York instead of San Francisco?

In life, it's tempting to ponder the roads not taken, but it is ultimately unproductive because it is impossible to determine where they might have led. In venture capital, however, you can and should track the outcomes of the investments you did not make because you can clearly identify what you missed out on. This process is commonly known as building your "anti-portfolio," and it can be a very valuable way of refining your due diligence process over time because the investments you *did not* make are more important than the ones that you *did*. If an equity investment results in a suboptimal outcome, the worst that can happen is it goes to zero and you lose 1x the money you invested (and your time). However, if an equity investment becomes a big winner, you could earn unlimited gains—sometimes early investments result in 1,000 or more times your money invested. Therefore, saying no to an opportunity with huge upside is actually worse for your returns than saying yes to something that never takes off.

Bessemer Venture Partners, one of the oldest venture capital firms in the country tracing its roots back to the Carnegie Steel fortune, popularized the concept of the anti-portfolio by publicly embracing their own failures and their resulting learnings on their website. They openly share stories about how they passed on companies like Airbnb (too expensive), Google (founders were too young), Tesla (negative margins), and Facebook (too much competition). In 2012, one of their partners even went so far as to tell Brian Armstrong, the founder of the crypto exchange Coinbase, which went public in 2021 at an $85.8 billion valuation, that there were no questions he could answer that would convince him to invest at a $10 million valuation.[1] Focusing on where your analysis of the opportunity may have broken down or been incorrect is an invaluable way of making it better over time.

Creating an anti-portfolio is a fun and valuable exercise for iterating on your decision-making process, but first you will have to actually make some decisions. In this section, we'll cover how to **analyze** investment opportunities to ensure you are making choices that will set you on a path to not only break into venture capital, but also to manufacture your own wild success once you make your way into the industry.

PRINCIPLE 4   Timing Is (Almost) Everything

PRINCIPLE 5   Money Matters

PRINCIPLE 6   Actively Manage Your Blind Spots

TIMING IS (ALMOST) EVERYTHING

Although my mother has been telling me that "timing is everything" my entire life, mostly in the context of analyzing my failed romantic relationships, I didn't believe it until I jumped headfirst into the world of technology and startups and I watched my first TED Talk. Glued to my laptop in a bustling coworking space in Hong Kong, gripping my noise-canceling headphones as close to my ears as possible, I could feel my perspective on the world shifting as I absorbed Bill Gross's viral six-and-a-half-minute speech, "The Single Biggest Reason Why Start-Ups Succeed."[1]

As the founder of Idealab, a Pasadena, California–based "startup studio" that has been starting and funding new business ideas since its establishment in 1996, it is certainly no surprise his talk is one of the most popular TED talks of all time. Bill Gross played a firsthand role in creating more than 150 businesses. As he prepared for Idealab's 20-year anniversary, Bill decided to analyze the biggest factor in each company's ultimate success or failure, and even he was surprised by the findings. Looking at the role of funding, business model, ideas, team, and timing, Bill determined that timing was by far the most important factor in the ultimate success or failure of the business. In fact, it was the key determinant in 42 percent of cases.

I heard about the importance of timing firsthand from my partner at SemperVirens Venture Capital, Caribou Honig. Although I know his story well through our work together, I had the privilege of formally interviewing him about timing for this book to really dig into the details. Although Caribou is now widely recognized as a successful venture investor, he had no experience in the venture capital world when he and several of his former colleagues from a data-driven finance firm called Capital One decided to start QED, a fintech-focused venture capital firm, in 2008. Since their founding, QED has minted billions on winning investments like Credit Karma (bought by Intuit for $8.1 billion), SoFi (went public via SPAC at $8.7 billion), and Nubank (last valued at $41.5 billion).

> "Timing" is just another way of expressing the idea that the world must be ready for what a company is offering, and there usually needs to be an external catalyst for widespread adoption.

His eyes glistened with the satisfaction of hindsight as he recalled in our interview how timing played a critical role in the success of their biggest investments as well as in the ultimate success of the firm itself. "Just months after we founded QED, the Great Financial Crisis hit. The incumbent financial giants were retreating on multiple fronts, thus creating great opportunities for startups to gain new market share. Generalist venture capital funds were reluctant to invest in the sector at the time given the economic pullback, which opened a unique opportunity for QED to invest into the Fintech thesis. We were lucky in that the timing was set to be perfect. It was good fortune, not good strategy," he said.

In most cases, "timing" is just another way of expressing the idea that the world must be ready for what a company is offering, and there usually needs to be an external catalyst for widespread adoption. Even if a startup has built something truly amazing and innovative, it is more often macroeconomic factors like the overall economy, gas prices, inflation, or unemployment rates that truly catalyze widespread adoption of a new technology, product, or service.

External factors that benefit a startup's growth are referred to as **tailwinds** because they impact a business trajectory similarly to how wind blowing in the direction of an aircraft helps increase its speed, regardless of the skill of the pilot. By contrast, **headwinds** inevitably slow down a business by adding resistance to its natural path.

Two of the most cited examples of epic tailwinds in venture capital are Airbnb and Uber. Founded in 2008 and 2009 respectively, most venture investors were focused on public perception as critical headwinds to mass adoption of their products. The prevailing wisdom was that even if consumers were unsatisfied with the prices and experience of existing alternatives like hotels and taxis, there would never be a critical supply of home renters or drivers because most people did not want strangers staying in their homes or riding in their cars with them. However, in 2008, when the Financial Crisis and the Great Recession left millions of Americans unemployed and in desperate need of supplemental income, they were more than willing to earn a few extra dollars by renting out a room or giving a stranger a ride. Suddenly, the direction of the wind shifted, and significant tailwinds led to the meteoric rise of two of the most valuable and transformative businesses in recent history.

When it comes to analyzing an investment opportunity, timing may ultimately be the most important, but it can often feel like it is beyond your control and therefore hard to analyze. After all, most billion-dollar businesses are built over the course of 5 to 10 years, and the headwinds or tailwinds at play when you are conducting due diligence may shift significantly in the future. While there are certainly elements of timing that are beyond one's control, a thorough due diligence process takes other key factors into consideration that will give you insight into how a given investment is likely to perform. Your analysis must ensure that before making an investment, a company has as many other things going for it as possible. This will provide them with the ability to withstand market dynamics long enough to find good timing.

A thorough due diligence process takes five key factors into consideration—in total, I call these the 5 Ts. We'll start by diving into the framework itself, and then we will circle back to how you can leverage the process to choose investments that are likely to have the best possible timing for success.

THE 5 Ts

When I was just breaking into the venture world, I was eager to connect with other female investors who had blazed a path ahead of me. One of my former bosses connected me to a friend of his named Alicia who was a prolific angel investor in New York, and on my next overseas trip from Asia, I found myself sitting across from her at a popular hotel restaurant and bar in SoHo, marveling at her effortless confidence and glamour. A former finance executive turned startup investor, Alicia had multiple Ivy League degrees, held several board seats, and was a frequent guest on CNBC to talk about her investment style and the rise of venture capital's importance in the economy. Relieved to finally have another woman to talk to, I admitted to her that I was suffering from major imposter syndrome and struggling with needing to project an air of confidence and expertise when I was only getting started as an investor at Fresco Capital.

As one of the only women investing in startups in Asia, I was often asked to sit on panels or judge startup competitions, and I found myself at a loss for what to say as I was still figuring out my own process for analyzing investments. Alicia smiled and assured me that all I needed was to create my own **due diligence checklist**, or a set of questions I could keep in my back pocket to bring me confidence when I was evaluating a startup or sitting on a judging panel.

Inspired by Atul Gawande's bestseller *The Checklist Manifesto*, creating a simple but repeatable process in the form of a checklist could help me deal with the increasing complexity of analyzing the quality of an innovative business in an uncertain world. Gawande highlights in his book that regardless of how much of an expert you may be, a well-designed checklist can improve outcomes in everything from surgery to disaster relief. And now, venture capital.

The 5 Ts will also help you properly invest your time, keep your deal flow prioritized, and stay true to your investment thesis.

Alicia generously shared her diligence checklist with me that day, which I furiously noted as a list of several questions and scribbled them in my beat-up black Moleskine notebook. They became an essential guidepost for many of my diligence conversations in my early days of venture investing. Over the years, I have evolved these questions, primarily to include alliteration so that I don't forget them, but the core idea remains unchanged: accurately, efficiently, and consistently analyzing investment opportunities is a critical step in creating lucky outcomes. In addition to streamlining your decision-making process, the 5 Ts will also help you properly invest your time, keep your deal flow prioritized, and stay true to your investment thesis.

For nearly a decade, I have evaluated thousands of investment opportunities based on five key factors: Team, Technology, TAM, Terms, and (of course) Timing. Regardless of the stage, industry, geography, and founder profile you are targeting in your investment thesis, these diligence categories will help you analyze and select the best opportunities that are most likely to lead to massive success in venture. Every new business starts with one or more founders coming up with a new idea, so let's begin with the importance of the team.

TEAM

Pop culture makes building a billion-dollar business look like a roller coaster, but the kind you'd ride for thrills at an amusement park. Hit TV shows like HBO's *Silicon Valley* satirizing the rise of a fictional startup, Showtime's depiction of the rise and fall of Travis Kalanick as the cofounder and CEO of Uber in *Super Pumped*, or Aaron Sorkin and David Fincher's Oscar-winning film *The Social Network* about Mark Zuckerberg's dramatic transformation from nerdy outcast to powerful billionaire, the startup journey is depicted as a glamorous one, filled with spontaneous strokes of genius, celebrity-filled parties, and heroic persistence against the establishment. Having now been part of hundreds of startup journeys as an investor, advisor, and friend, I can assure you these dramatic depictions squarely belong in the world of fiction. In reality, founding a trailblazing, life-changing, global powerhouse business is a harrowing ride filled with countless unexpected turns that twist your stomach, test your understanding of physics, and completely throw off your center of gravity. Although it can often feel like the ultimate outcome of a business is out of a founder's control, there are millions of active choices that lead to the formation of a founding team, and a million more choices that founding team makes every day that add up to the eventual result.

This is precisely why evaluation of a founding team is an essential part of the due diligence process:

Why are they starting this business?

Why are they in the best position to win when others inevitably pursue the same opportunity or build competing solutions to the same problem?

Will they stick around when things grow difficult and nobody is around to pat them on the back or tell them they are doing a good job?

How will they handle the business when an economic crisis hits, they lose a customer, or the product breaks down? It's impossible to know what will happen over the lifetime of a business, but it is possible to at least preliminarily predict how a leader might navigate those challenges.

When we analyze the founding team of a prospective investment, we dig into their past experiences, professional accomplishments, internal and external motivations, and even their personal lives to understand how they will navigate the inevitable ups and downs of building a billion-dollar business. Most great founders are impressive storytellers. They have carefully crafted their personal narratives, and they have likely spent hundreds of hours building pitch decks to help paint a vision of their transformative business. These materials are a great place to start, but we must dig beneath the surface to predict what types of choices these founders will make over time.

Remember that founders have carefully crafted their personal narratives, and they have likely spent hundreds of hours building pitch decks to help paint a vision of their transformative business.

We always start our analysis by asking the team about these future challenges directly. We also rely on who we know to add depth to our understanding of the quality of the team. We ask founders for personal and professional references that can speak to their experiences, but we also rely deeply on our personal networks for back-channel references who can provide unfiltered insight into their true colors.

Who has worked with them before and watched them make these choices in real time?

Who can corroborate their narratives?

The best back-channel references I have heard include things like, "If I could hire her again, I would do it in a heartbeat," or "Within our entire portfolio, he is the best CEO I have ever worked with." The worst have included, "She's got a lot of energy, but she is not detail oriented," or a doozie, "I wouldn't touch that guy with a 10-foot pole."

We then compile these direct and indirect sources of information into a comprehensive picture of the team. Here are the questions I typically look to answer when evaluating a team during a diligence process:

- **How strong is their founder/market fit? Do they have personal experience with the problem they are solving? Why do they care?** This helps us understand their motivations and their ability to navigate the unique complexities of their market.

- **Besides the cofounders and CEO, who is on the team?** What are their respective areas of expertise, and are they complementary to each other? Do they work well together? This helps paint a picture of what the leadership team will look like over time and how they might navigate key strategy decisions when not everyone agrees on the right path forward.

- **Are there any key gaps on the founding team that they need to fill in the near future in order to be successful?** These gaps could include things like technical talent, sales leadership, operational expertise, or industry connections. If they exist, how is the team addressing those gaps? This is usually an indicator of the team's self-awareness and ability to ask for help when they need it most.

- **Is this CEO able to attract resources?** This is a clear indicator of their ability to fundraise and to recruit top talent, both of which are necessary in order to succeed long-term.

- **Can they admit their mistakes? What are examples of times they have been wrong, and how have they adapted?** It will be impossible to always make the right choices when building a business, and the ability to recognize a bad choice and pivot accordingly is critical.

- **Have they led a team or a company before?** Do they know what it is like to experience hypergrowth and all of the challenges that come with that? Past performance is not necessarily an indicator of future success, but it helps to have a baseline of experience to draw from.

- **What kind of relationship do they want with their investors?** Are they looking for a collaborative partnership or just a transaction? There is no right answer here, as there are all different styles of investing, but it will help you figure out if you have similar expectations from each other as the business evolves over time.

- **How do they define success?** What are they hoping to achieve, and is it in line with what we believe is an exciting outcome? As we have discussed, most venture capital funds need at least a few companies that earn them 100x or more on their money. Is that the type of return that the founder is looking for too? It helps to make sure that expectations are completely aligned, even if it seems like it should be obvious.

During the process of seeking answers to these questions, I often feel more like a psychologist or a detective than an investor, but analyzing what lies beneath the surface is precisely what creates the proper conditions for success in venture capital. Painting a comprehensive picture of the founding team and how they make choices equips you with a strong foundation for analyzing how they may navigate different external factors that ultimately lead to "good timing" or "bad timing."

TECHNOLOGY

Since most venture investments are in companies that are selling technology products, as opposed to physical goods or business services, it is important to assess how unique, how transformative, and how defensible the company's product really is. What does this business do that has never been done before, and how much does that really matter? In some cases, there are deep technology innovations that include completely new inventions like quantum computing, self-guided artificial intelligence, new medical devices, or new pharmaceutical treatments. This process of creating a completely new capability can be very lucrative, but the diligence process requires having the technical knowledge yourself or direct access to a trusted reference or experts who can help you discern whether or not this new technology actually works as well as when it might be commercially viable.

In most other cases, there are simply *new technology applications* that merely leverage existing capabilities to solve new problems. This leads to a slightly different diligence process as it is important to ensure that their technology works as intended, but it is not necessarily the technology itself that is the big bet. For example, I have invested in companies leveraging artificial intelligence to ask users simple questions and determine what type of healthcare they need based on their responses. Or companies using data science to collect information about job-seekers to determine in what types of jobs, teams, or companies they are most likely to succeed. In these cases, the technology portion of my due diligence process mostly involved testing the product and ensuring it does what it is supposed to do (and does it well). Did the product *actually* give me accurate recommendations for my healthcare needs, or did it merely deliver random information that left me no better off than I was before?

When assessing the technology component—the core innovation enabling this business—you are trying to determine if this business can leverage technology to deliver the outcomes that it promises. Here's what I ask to analyze this component of a prospective investment:

- **What is truly unique about this product or business, and has it ever been done in this way before? If not, why not?** This will provide a glimpse into how the technology and timing will interplay to create long-term success (or not).

- **What problem is this product solving for its customers, and how important is that problem?** Is it a "nice to have" or a "need to have"? If the technology is solving a mission-critical problem—or an issue that is essential to the success or survival of its customers—it is far more likely that customers will start using it and paying for it immediately and the company will increase in value as a result.

- **How much better is this solution for that problem than the existing alternatives?** Is technology making it a little bit better or a lot better? If there is another way of solving the problem at hand, there needs to be sufficient motivation for customers to change their current behavior. Most people won't make a change for a 10 percent improvement, for example, but they definitely will for a 10-times improvement.

- **Does this product actually do what it says it does?** Obviously, customers won't buy something that doesn't actually work as intended. It may seem obvious, but entrepreneurs are known for making big claims. It's good practice to double-check that they are true, or else you will end up with a massive scandal on your hands.

- **How unique is this technology?** How hard would it be for another company to create something similar and sell to the same market? What is preventing them from doing that? Understanding competing solutions, even if not exactly the same, is important for determining how a business might grow over time and how big the opportunity really is.

- **Who on the team oversees developing, maintaining, and improving this technology over time?** Even if the technology is both viable and unique right now, the company will need to continually evolve the product over the next 5 to 10 years to maintain their competitive edge. Do they have the right people involved to do that?

Looking back on most successful investments during his time investing at QED, Caribou noted that properly analyzing the technology component of a business was a critical step in determining how defensible a product really is. In other words, is the company's product likely to withstand competition over time, or will they lose their customers after a few months or years? In his top 12 performing investments, Caribou credited only three with a cutting-edge technology that ultimately led to their success. For the other big winners, their product was more a result of business model or product innovation than a new technology itself. "There are lots of different ways to create defensibility, whether it's a sweetheart deal with a supplier, the product's ability to solve for a lot of different problems simultaneously, or bespoke predictive models based on proprietary data sets," he told me, "It doesn't need to be *just* technology, per se."

In either case, properly analyzing the viability of an opportunity requires teasing out what is actually driving the quality of the product that is being sold (technology innovation or something else). It is only then that you can start to understand how timing might play a role in the company's ultimate success or failure.

TOTAL ADDRESSABLE MARKET (TAM)

Commonly referred to as TAM, total addressable market is a high-level calculation of the potential revenue opportunity of a business if they were able to achieve 100 percent market share. In other words, if every single person or business in your target market bought this product, how much money could you make? Of course, it is impossible to achieve perfect market penetration, but the TAM calculation is a way to deduce how big and valuable a problem a company is solving. If everything were to go right, how big could this company possibly be?

TAM is a particularly important part of the diligence process because venture capital is governed by the power law, meaning that any single investment can and will have an exponential effect on your overall returns. As Peter Thiel points out in his book with Blake Masters, *Zero to One: Notes on Startups or How to Build the Future*, "The biggest secret in venture capital is that the best investment in a successful fund equals or outperforms the entire rest of the fund."

Sebastian Mallaby dives deeper into the concept in his most recent book, *The Power Law: Venture Capital and the Making of the New Future*, where he explains precisely why VCs need to swing for the fences with every investment—because outcomes don't follow a normal distribution of returns. Instead, a small proportion of outcomes drive the bulk of returns, and winners advance at an accelerating and exponential rate. This is validated by decades of historical data. Take, for example, Y Combinator, the startup accelerator that has backed hundreds of companies since its foundation in 2005. As of 2012, they calculated that 75 percent of their gains came from only 2 of their 280 investments in the previous seven years.[2]

This means that when you are evaluating any single investment, you need to believe that it can and will have an exponential effect on your overall returns. You must be looking for 100x or even 1,000x returns, not just 2x or 3x. In fact, if every one of your investments returned 2x or 3x, you would not be considered successful in venture capital at all. As Mallaby put it in his book, "When today's venture capitalists back flying cars or space tourism or artificial intelligence systems that write film scripts, they are following this power-law logic. Their job is to look over the horizon to reach for high-risk, huge-reward possibilities that most people believe to be unreachable."[3]

These extremely high growth returns are generated by companies that sell for billions or multiple billions of dollars, implying they have annual revenues of $100 million or more. Calculating TAM is an important part of analyzing the potential upside of a given investment because there are hundreds and thousands of businesses established every year that just don't have the potential to grow to that size and scale. For example, let's say you are deciding whether to fund a company that sells scheduling and customer communication tools to watch repair professionals. Sounds like a unique idea—watches break all the time! The team is very impressive, and your diligence process determines that the technology is sound and innovative—it has never been built before. As you turn your attention to TAM, you begin researching the market and discover that, according to the Bureau of Labor Statistics, there are 2,430 watch repair professionals in the United States.[4] In order to earn $100 million in revenues per year, this company would need to charge every watch repair professional at least $40,000 per year. The median salary of a watch repair professional is only $48,000 per year, which makes it unlikely they'd be able to spend this amount of money on anything, let alone a piece of software.

Instead, it seems likely they could only charge $1,000 per year, which would result in a total addressable market of $1,000 \times 2,480 = \$2,480,000$. This is a far cry from the billion or multibillion-dollar opportunities that are likely to drive grand slam investments, making this particular company likely not worth your time or capital, even if every other part of the business passes your diligence checklist. Most entrepreneurs will provide you with a calculation of TAM, but due diligence is all about validating these assumptions, and it's important to run your own process to determine the magnitude of the investment at hand.

Here are some guiding questions to determine TAM as you analyze the potential upside for a given business:

- During the technology component of the diligence checklist, you homed in on *what* problem this product is solving. Now, you must pay attention to exactly how much money is being spent every year solving this problem. Even if potential customers aren't buying the product you are evaluating during diligence, getting a sense of how much they are spending on other solutions will help you figure out if the target customer even has the capital to spend on a better solution in the first place.

- Who is the person or business that will be paying for this product? This needs to be specific—what type of person (age, demographic, income range) or what type of business (company size, industry, location, revenue or budget) is the company targeting? How many of these types of people or businesses exist in the world? This gets at the *total* part of *total addressable market.*

- If targeting businesses, who within that company will be making the purchasing decision, and what budget will they be drawing from to pay for it? How big are those budgets? These specifics matter a lot when determining the actual *addressable* part of TAM.

- When looking at overall budgets, and how much money customers spend on solving this problem, what would a likely annual contract value (ACV) be for this business? If selling to individuals, this would merely be the price tag of the product. This will guide you toward the *market* size of TAM.

TERMS

When you make a venture capital investment in a company, you are trading your money for a stake in a business (or a future business). **Terms** are the details of the agreement that you sign dictating the details of what you are putting in (money) and what you are getting in return (equity shares in the company). More important, terms also outline how money flows back to you in the case of an exit, a change in control, or a liquidation of the company. When it comes to getting money back from your investments, the devil is in the details, and those details are written out in the many pages of legalese that you will be asked to sign when you complete your investment. Typically, these terms of negotiated between the **lead investor** and the **CEO**, and the rest of the **coinvestors** can merely choose whether to accept or reject the deal.

Although terms are by far the most boring part of the diligence process, they are an essential component to assessing the likelihood of various potential outcomes because they are the guardrails that will guide the decisions that founders and other investors will make over time. You can't predict exactly what will happen in the future, but you can do the work to deduce what economically rational actors will do when faced with certain choices.

I was recently advising a company in my portfolio as they navigated an acquisition offer from a competing company. The acquirer offered to buy the company for $55 million. Although this number may seem high, the startup had raised $75 million in capital from investors since it was established. When we invested, the terms of the deal included a **2x liquidation preference**, meaning all investors needed to be repaid at least twice their initial investment before any of the proceeds went to founders. That meant that the founding team— the people who were tasked with negotiating the acquisition—stood to receive nothing from the transaction unless the acquirer increased their price to $150 million or more (a very unlikely scenario). This left the CEO very unmotivated to try to get the best price possible, so he simply accepted the first offer instead of trying to get a better price.

The lead investor who negotiated these terms was likely merely trying to ensure their own interests with clever terms, but perhaps did not consider realistically how it would impact economic incentives in the event of an exit. As a VC, even if you are not the one negotiating detailed terms, it is important during your due diligence to dig into the details of what you are signing and what it means for the likelihood of potential outcomes in the future. Terms are critical components to assessing the likelihood of various potential outcomes.

When making a venture capital investment in a company, two primary structures are used, each with a unique set of terms to consider: convertible notes and priced equity rounds.

Convertible notes are typically used to raise capital at the very early (pre-seed or seed stage) or very late stage (pre-IPO) of a company's life cycle; a convertible note is a technically a *short-term loan* that converts into equity upon a future financing. The most common type of convertible financing is a **SAFE note**, which stands for "Simple Agreement for Future Equity." This type of investment was introduced by the startup accelerator Y Combinator in 2013 to help founders standardize terms and ensure they weren't unknowingly locking themselves into overly onerous investment terms, which was historically a common occurrence for pre-revenue businesses.[5] Whether it is a standardized template like a SAFE, or a convertible note negotiated between a lead investor and a founder, there are several key terms to look for when analyzing the terms of this type of investment:

- **CONVERSION MILESTONES.** When and how will this loan convert into equity? Typically terms will dictate a conversion will happen on a particular date, also known as a **maturity date**, or at the time of a **qualified financing** or another fundraising event of a designated size (say, at least $5 million). Usually you are looking for milestones that are far enough into the future that the company can make real progress on the business, but not so far into the future that they may be incentivized to continue raising money on convertible notes instead of equity, in which case you could end up highly diluted. Typical maturity dates range from 18 to 24 months, and qualified financings are, on average, $2 million or more.

- **INTEREST RATE.** Because a convertible note is technically a debt instrument, it often includes an interest rate that accrues between the time of investment and the conversion milestone. However, instead of receiving the accrued interest in cash, the amount is also converted to equity at the time of conversion. Because VCs are usually looking for 100x returns, the interest rate is usually negligible, and it is increasingly common for this term to be left out altogether. Be wary of interest rates that are extremely high as they may indicate that the lead investor is not looking for the same long-term upside that you are.

- **VALUATION CAP.** A convertible note is not technically an equity investment; it is a loan, so you do not receive shares in the company at the time of the financing. Instead, you agree on a valuation cap or the maximum dollar amount that will be used to calculate how much of the business you receive at the time of conversion.

$$\text{Ownership \%} = \frac{\begin{array}{cc}\$ \text{ you} & \text{accrued interest} \\ \text{invested} & + & \text{if applicable}\end{array}}{\begin{array}{c}\text{The valuation cap, or the valuation} \\ \text{at the time of financing, whichever is lower}\end{array}}$$

- **DISCOUNT RATE.** In some cases, convertible notes include discount rates, in addition to or in place of a valuation cap, used to calculate the value of an investment at time of conversion. This is the valuation discount you would receive relative to the other investors in a subsequent financing. In cases where there is both a valuation cap and a discount rate, you would receive the lower of the two at the time of conversion. A typical acceptable discount rate ranges from 10 to 25 percent, and anything higher or lower warrants a conversation with founders or lead investors on what their expectations are for the timing, amount, and value of future financings.

- **LIQUIDATION PREFERENCE.** This term outlines how and when you will get paid back in the event there is some sort of change in control (merger, acquisition, bankruptcy, or IPO) of the business before conversion occurs. A 1x liquidation preference means you get the amount of money you invested before any other shareholders get their first dollar; 2x means you get twice your money back, and so on. Liquidation preferences above 1x are unusual and can lead to distorted incentives, as I shared in the story earlier in the chapter.

Convertible notes have increased in popularity as a way for founders to raise money quickly and efficiently without needing to deal with the time-consuming and resource intensive process of determining a valuation. Because they are relatively simple, straightforward, and tend to align with generally accepted industry standards as outlined by the SAFE, they have also served to make early stage investing more accessible to new investors. The major drawback is that they introduce additional uncertainty since you are not receiving shares at the time of investment, and the valuation at which you will receive the shares is not technically guaranteed.

Priced equity rounds, on the other hand, are more formal financings that actually create new equity shares for issue to investors at the time of financing. Therefore, you officially become a shareholder in the business and you know exactly how many shares you are receiving and for what price. Similar to any other type of financing, the terms of the share offering are typically negotiated between the lead investor and the CEO, and coinvestors can choose whether or not to accept these terms. When analyzing the terms of a priced round, the goal is the same as a convertible note financing—to determine how these terms will incentivize behavior in the future. The main terms you will want to assess are:

- **VALUATION.** The valuation of the company at the time of financing is how much it is worth and is a critical component in calculating how much of the business you own as a result of your investment. Although the term "valuation" is thrown around quite often, it is important to distinguish between pre-money and post-money valuations. **Pre-money valuation** is how much the company is worth *at the time of the financing*. In other words, how much value has this company created up until the moment of this share offering? **Post-money valuation** is how much the company is worth *once the financing is complete*. This is important because the cash raised as part of the investment is considered an asset, and therefore actually adds to the equity value of the business. We will dive deeper into ownership in the next chapter, but it is important to note that it is calculated using post-money valuation:

  Post-money valuation = Pre-money valuation + round size (see following bullet point)

  $$\text{Ownership \%} = \frac{\$ \text{ you invested}}{\text{Post-money valuation}}$$

- **ROUND SIZE.** How much money is the company raising in this financing? Usually a term sheet will dictate the minimum and maximum amount of money that can be raised. Although raising more money can be helpful by extending the timeline until the company will need to raise additional capital and can help CEOs grow the business faster with the additional cash in their coffers, it also means that the post-money valuation is higher, so your ownership percentage is actually lower. Ask yourself what are the risks and benefits to the round size dictated in the term sheet—does it ultimately help or hurt the company's future growth trajectory to have a higher post-money valuation?

- **SECURITY.** An equity financing technically means that a company is creating new shares in the business that they then sell to you as the investor. The security type dictates what type of shares you will receive as part of this financing—*common shares* or *preferred shares*. Most founders and employees own common shares (also known as common stock), and most investors purchase preferred shares. Preferred shares have separate voting rights and get paid out first in the event of a liquidation.

- **VOTING RIGHTS.** In the case where certain events or decisions may require shareholder approval, the terms of an investment round dictate who votes on what and how many people need to vote yes for something to get approved. This process may seem obscure, but it applies to critical decisions like accepting or rejecting an acquisition offer, deciding to go for an IPO, removing a CEO, or declaring bankruptcy. Not all investors get voting rights with their investment, especially if you are investing a small amount, so it is important to consider how this may impact your ability to influence future outcomes of the business.

- **INFORMATION RIGHTS.** This term delineates who has access to key proprietary information about the company's performance. Typically this is determined by the size of investment, where *major investors* will have full information rights, but *minor investors* do not.

- **LIQUIDATION PREFERENCE.** The same definition from the convertible note applies here (see earlier discussion).

- **BOARD OF DIRECTORS.** Typically put in place at the time of the first priced equity round, the **board of directors** is the key governing body for a company charged with supervising the business, setting strategy, and making big decisions on behalf of the other shareholders. Technically, a board of directors is composed of representatives "chosen" by common stockholders (typically, the CEO and other key employees), representatives "chosen" by preferred stockholders (typically the lead investors from major financing rounds), and independent directors (experts or key advisors who are not investors in the company). In practice, the board of directors is usually composed of the largest shareholders in a business. Even if you are not planning to join the board as part of your investment, this term is important to consider because as Sarah Smith shared with us in Principle 2, it is not just the CEO but also the board of directors who hold the keys to major decisions around future financings. Besides the team you've analyzed so far, who are the other players who will be dictating the trajectory of the business going forward? What do they care about, and what kind of people are they? Even if you don't have enough information to diligence them personally, pay attention to the reputation of the largest shareholders as it can be a big clue to how they might behave in the future.

Just like an actor breaking into Hollywood or an athlete collecting championship rings, the terms of an agreement will sweeten with success, reputation, and past precedent. When you are breaking into venture and making your first investments, it is more than likely you will not be a lead investor, and the terms of the deal are the terms of the deal. It is merely up to you to decide whether to accept them. Even if you are a smaller investor, here are some steps you can take to get all the information you need to determine whether you're interested in accepting the terms.

- It may sound obvious, but especially if you are considering investing on a convertible note, confirm with the company that you are investing at the same terms as the lead investor and all other investors in the round. Although it is rare, it is technically possible to draft different agreements for different investors. If this is the case, it is a major red flag.

- Ask the CEO how and why they arrived at the key terms when negotiating with the lead investor. Even if they are not ideal, it is important to determine if a founder or CEO even understands what key terms may mean for the future of the business. If they don't know what the terms mean, or they imply they were strong-armed into accepting them, that could be a red flag to consider. After all, the process of raising money is merely a practice run for the process of negotiating a sale or preparing for an IPO. Does this team have the skills that make sure they are successful?

- Take the time to connect with the lead investor and/or the members of the board. As we discussed in Principle 2, you can only *read the air*, or in other words predict or influence outcomes in the future if you know the key players around the table. If they are not willing to meet with you or have clearly different incentives, that could be a red flag.

- If you can afford it, seek the advice of legal counsel (or merely ask an experienced friend or colleague) to review the investment terms on your behalf. Is there anything they see as unusual or alarming? It always helps to get a second pair of eyes, especially if you are just starting out and might not know what to look for.

FINALLY, TIMING

Now that you've been able to analyze the team, technology, TAM, and terms of your potential investment, you are fully equipped to turn your attention back to market timing. Assuming your analysis demonstrates that the business has as many other positive factors at play as possible, it is up to you to determine how and what headwinds and tailwinds are likely to influence the ultimate outcome of your investment. Similar to a surfer who cannot control the waves but can anticipate their rhythm and strength in order to determine the right moment to get up and ride them, you must analyze the most likely timing for key catalysts or accelerants for your potential investment's growth trajectory.

In Principle 3, I discussed my investment thesis around the future of work and how my interest in the growing need for mental health-care helped my network introduce me to a company called Spring Health, a data-driven mental healthcare solution that employers can purchase and provide to their employees alongside their traditional healthcare benefits. I first met April Koh when she was starting her first round of financing. Many other investors believed that although she and her team had built an impressive technology product in a market with a big TAM, and the terms were acceptable, market timing was such that it would take a very long time for the company to grow to scale. When I was advocating my firm at the time make an investment in the business, one of the general partners asked me, "Mental health . . . I mean, is that really a thing? I've never had any issues with it, so I don't know why employers would really care."

As an older millennial who has benefitted from a growing cultural acceptance of mental health challenges and a roster of therapists since my teens, it seemed like an absolute no-brainer to me that general healthcare benefits should expand from physical health to also include mental health, and that a growing contingent of employees would soon be demanding this type of care from their employer-sponsored health plans. Although the exact timing wasn't clear, I did know that millennials like me were starting to make up more and more of the workforce every year. In fact, as of 2016, one in three workers was a millennial, the largest generation in the labor force at the time.[6] This process of a new generation gaining power, authority, and influence is known as a **demographic shift**, and it can be a major tailwind for new innovation.

Furthermore, I was also seeing popular culture start to pay more attention to mental health. Instead of vilifying celebrities who had mental breakdowns or suffered from depression or anxiety, the media was starting to pull back the curtain on the details of these challenges. More and more of my friends and colleagues talked about their own struggles. Big names like Prince Harry, Selena Gomez, Mariah Carey, Lady Gaga, and Oprah Winfrey started to discuss what it was like for them to experience mental health challenges, as well as share best practices on getting help. This type of cultural zeitgeist is another big tailwind for disruption, and I had a feeling it could serve as a catalyst for making mental healthcare more accessible and ubiquitous.

Finally, in 2020 as the Covid-19 pandemic hit, mental health surged to the forefront of the national consciousness. Thousands of people were dying every day, the stock market lost one-quarter of its value in less than a week, and unemployment surged to its highest rates since the Great Depression. Frontline workers in healthcare, retail, and manufacturing were either exposed to life-threatening risks at work every day or were sidelined and isolated at home wondering when they'd earn a paycheck again.

The World Health Organization cited a 25 percent increase in depression and anxiety, with women and young people bearing the brunt of the challenges.[7] Mental healthcare quickly became table stakes for employers to be providing to their employees, and investment in the category became obvious to most venture capitalists, even those who had been most doubtful just a year or two earlier. Spring

Health found itself growing exponentially, with revenues exploding and their valuation increasing to several billion dollars in a matter of months. Although these types of **economic shocks** are often beyond our control, they also serve as bittersweet tailwinds for the adoption of new and different ways of doing things.

Here are some key questions I use for analyzing market timing:

- **What are the current barriers to adoption and constraints to growth for this business?** In other words, what are the main reasons this market has not yet been disrupted? Once you can identify why an investment might not work, you can turn your attention to what might change or remove those barriers to adoption.

- **What conditions must be met for consumers or businesses to become customers?** What could contribute to these conditions becoming true? This can help you identify what type of catalysts to adoption to look for in your further analysis of market timing.

- **How might demographic shifts impact the customer base of this business?** Is the target customer cohort growing or shrinking in size? Is their power and ability to make purchasing decisions increasing or decreasing over time?

- **How do popular culture and the media regard the problem this business is solving?** Is popular opinion shifting in one direction or another? Perhaps we are in the midst of a **cultural zeitgeist** that could influence adoption of a new innovation.

- **How does government policy impact the growth of this business?** Are there any **policy changes** up for consideration or top of mind for lawmakers that could put incentives or disincentives in place in the near future?

- **What is the likelihood of an economic shock in the next 5 to 10 years, and how would that impact this business?**

Would a recession increase or decrease demand for this product?

In many cases, like the rise of innovation in financial technology post–Financial Crisis or the widespread adoption of mental healthcare benefits during the Covid-19 pandemic, "good timing" is merely the acceleration of an already inevitable trend. Cultural, demographic, political, or economic changes pour fuel on a smoldering fire and turn it into a full-scale blaze. Neither you as an investor nor the CEO of the business you are investing in can control the exact timing of these trends. However, a thorough market analysis and due diligence process will ensure you have the right information to determine how likely it is that your investment will result in extreme success.

BREAKTHROUGH TIPS FOR GETTING TIMING RIGHT

- Get to know the founding team beyond just the stories they tell during the fundraising process. Leverage your network and remember to back-channel to create a comprehensive picture of how the company leadership makes decisions and how they are likely to behave in both good times and bad.

- Dive into the details of the technology and leverage your own experience as well as that of experts in your network to analyze how special the product is.

- Do the math to figure out exactly how big this investment could possibly get. Remember that the power law dictates returns, and you need to swing for the fences in order to truly be successful as a venture capital investor.

- Remember that when it comes to getting money back from your investments, the devil is in the details.

- Make sure you understand the terms of the financing and how they may impact you in a variety of scenarios.

- Identify what factors are likely to influence market timing over the life span of this business, and how they will impact the growth trajectory of the company.

- Keep track of your analysis of each of these factors, your ultimate investment decision, and the eventual outcome of the business so you can review and iterate upon your process over time.

MONEY MATTERS

As a 20-year-old intern at Goldman Sachs, soaking in the wonders of Wall Street culture, I was naturally terrified by my superiors. One of the senior leaders in my division, whom I'll call Pat, would walk up and down the trading floor and, as if choreographed perfectly, the moment he would walk by, everyone would look down or pick up a phone in order to appear very busy concentrating on being amazing at their jobs. An ex–soccer player, Pat would swagger up and down the aisles, using various intimidation tactics to make sure everyone knew he was the top dog. He once told me never to look him in the eyes. Another time he asked me what I thought of his Rolex watch, and when I started to reply, he simply told me, "Shut the fuck up." Despite this comical yet wholly unacceptable abuse, I am very grateful to Pat for teaching me one of the most important lessons of my career: money matters.

Given I wasn't supposed to talk or look him in the eyes, I was nervous when Pat called me into his office one day late in the summer. His monochrome blue eyes were devoid of any discernible emotion. His Long Island accent and alpha male manner of leaning back in his chair made it clear that he was judging me but also cared very little about this interaction. Without any small talk to warm up the conversation, he asked directly, "Why do you want to work at Goldman Sachs?"

Unsure of myself, I did my best to muster authentic confidence and draw upon answers I had rehearsed at various points in my internship. The memory is so overpowered by my own emotions of fear and confusion that I can't remember my exact words that day, but they were somewhat to the effect of, "I want to work at Goldman Sachs because I want to learn from the smartest people in the world. I want to understand how the most important system in our lives—the financial system—works. I want to serve our clients to the best of my ability. I really want to change the world one day, and I think this is the best place to get started."

He stared at me, completely unmoved, and shook his head. "I don't believe you. You're lying." I froze. He continued, "The only acceptable answer is that you are here because you want to make money. If anybody ever tells you otherwise, they're lying to you, they're lying to themselves, or both. Either way, you can't trust them."

I snapped into compliance and agreed, and ultimately ended up with a job at the firm, but it took years for my initial disillusionment to mature into acceptance and understanding.

As much as I did want to change the world, I also knew that earning $70,000 my first year out of college in the early 2000s would enable me to support myself and launch a financially independent life. I also knew that the prospect of making millions of dollars before I was 30—something very common on Wall Street at the time—meant I would open myself up to many exciting options in life and in my career that extended well beyond Goldman Sachs. Working in a creative industry, public service, or pursuing entrepreneurship would all become possibilities. So, yes, Pat was right. I wanted to make money. Of course, I also wanted to work with smart people, learn new things, and set myself up on a trajectory to do something meaningful with my life, but earning a solid income put me in an even better position to do all of those things too.

Whether it's Wall Street or Sand Hill Road, making money is always a primary motivation, whether people are willing to admit it or not. Although Silicon Valley is known for grandiose mission statements about saving the world, it's important to be aware that technology, and the funding behind it, is ultimately driven by profits. That does not negate the world-changing potential of the businesses being built, of course. In fact, solid business models with strong growth trajectories have incredible potential to transform our lives. However, being honest about your own motivations, and recognizing what drives others, facilitates alignment of incentives and makes rational behavior easier to predict. When there is a fork in the road, what choices are different stakeholders likely to make? How do their potential payouts incentivize them to behave? At the end of the day, successfully breaking into venture capital requires breaking down who makes how much on what and when, especially you. Unfortunately, though, in venture capital, it's harder than it seems to predict how much money you will make.

> Whether it's Wall Street or Sand Hill Road, making money is always a primary motivation, whether people are willing to admit it or not.

TO PROFIT OR NOT TO PROFIT?

Danielle Strachman, cofounder and general partner at 1517 Fund, experienced the power of profits firsthand because she started her venture capital career as a nonprofit. Before she cofounded 1517 Fund, Danielle gave away money to entrepreneurs as part of her role as director of the Thiel Fellowship, billionaire cofounder of PayPal Peter Thiel's philanthropic foundation. These grants were designed to provide founders with the resources they needed to take a leap of faith and start a business or pursue a new idea instead of taking a more traditional path through education and work. The Thiel Fellowship asked nothing in return of the founders—it was a grant, not an investment. After two years of giving away money and seeing some of these founders start to build large and profitable companies, Danielle started to wonder, "What if we were actually getting equity in these businesses in return for our cash?"

After doing the math, she realized that the $1.75 million they had granted to founders over the past few years would have been worth $35 million if they had simply asked for ownership in exchange for the money. Not only that, but she felt she would have had a better relationship with founders if she were a shareholder in the business. She told me in one of our many long, winding conversations over Zoom, "When we were a nonprofit, we felt good about what we were doing, but my incentives as an investor and a shareholder are totally different now. I am not on the sidelines; I am going to go the extra mile to help a company no matter what it takes. And founders treat us differently when we are owners in their companies. They talk to us differently—they go the extra mile, too."

As Danielle discovered, having ownership in a business completely changed the dynamic between her and the founders she was working with. Suddenly, they were not just friends and supporters, but collaborators working toward the same goal with fates intertwined. That meant that being an investor changed the way founders listened to her, responded to her feedback, and followed up on her requests. In other words, she found that investing yielded not only ownership but also power.

One of the things that surprised me the most about venture capital was the fact that you can access the best investment opportunities; you can analyze a team, technology, market, and set of potential outcomes with perfect accuracy; and you can even add a ton of value to a business, and *still* not make any money from your investment. This has happened to me more times than I can count. As a VC, your own cash flow is much harder to analyze than the cash flow of your potential investments. The business model of venture capital is not as straightforward as charging customers for a product. Instead, it is rooted in **ownership**. You make money based on how much of each company *your fund* owns, as well as how much of your fund *you* own.

In this chapter, we'll dive into how to make sure accessing and analyzing the best startup investments results in you *making money* as a venture capitalist.

Here's how to do that:

1. Get clear on your own business model as a VC.

2. Understand why ownership drives returns.

3. Avoid two key pitfalls when negotiating ownership.

STEP 1

GET CLEAR ON YOUR OWN BUSINESS MODEL AS A VC

One of the most exciting features of venture capital investments is that they have limited downside (the maximum you can lose is however much you invest), but unlimited upside (there is no maximum to how much you can make). However, it is important to recognize that how *you* make money in venture capital is determined by how your *fund* makes money, and in turn how you are compensated by the fund. If the fund doesn't earn profits, neither does anyone who works there, so let's start by quickly reviewing the business model of a venture capital *fund*.

As we outlined in the Introduction, there are two primary ways in which venture capital funds earn revenue:

1. **MANAGEMENT FEES.** The approximately 2 percent annual fee that the general partner charges the limited partners on their invested capital. These fees cover basic business costs like office space, salaries, and software. If you're hanging out in a coffee shop listening to VCs talk to each other, you might hear the common idiom, "Nobody is getting rich off of management fees." While management fees are helpful to keep food on the table and make sure all the trains run on time, they are somewhat negligible relative to the potential returns driven by carried interest.

2. **CARRIED INTEREST.** Commonly known as "carry," carried interest is a 20 percent fee earned by the general partner on any fund profits. You only make carry once you have returned all of your investor's initial capital. Once you've done that, you get to keep 20 percent of any and all upside earned from your investments. There is no limit to how much you make from your carry. This directly aligns your interests as a fund manager with the interests for your limited partners—the more money they make, the more money you make.

Upside for venture funds is driven by carried interest, but there are two big milestones you need to reach to start earning carried interest. First, you need your investments to return *cash* to your fund. This is commonly known as an *exit*, or a *liquidity event*—a sale, merger, acquisition, or IPO. When the fund receives this money back in exchange for its ownership in a company, the proceeds are then distributed back to your limited partners according to the size of their investment relative to the total size of the fund (so if I invest $5 million in a $10 million fund, I will get 50 percent of the total amount being returned to investors, less any applicable management fees).

What many may not realize is that getting *cash back* from your investments is different than your portfolio just getting *marked up*, which is when the underlying assets or the portfolio companies raise follow-on funding from other investors who value them at a higher amount than when you first invested. Markups are great because they are early indicators of long-term success and mean there is a higher likelihood that you will eventually earn money from that investment. However, markups are just **paper gains**, meaning they are not *actual* gains, and they unfortunately do not result in any kind of real compensation for you as a manager.

The second thing that needs to happen to start earning carry is that you need to return all of your investors' initial capital—also known as earning a 1x multiple or returning the fund. This means that you could have several exits and return money to your investors, but unless you return *enough* money to your investors first, you will still not see a penny yourself. For example, I was ecstatic when one of my first investments at Fresco Capital in a San Francisco–based education technology company called SchoolMint sold to a private equity firm only three years after I had made the initial investment! To keep the math simple, let's assume I had invested roughly $100,000 out of a $10 million fund. When the liquidity event occurred, the company was valued at more than 10x its initial valuation, allowing us to return something like $1 million in cash to our investors—a big win! But unfortunately not big enough, as we still had $9 million more to earn in profit before we were "in the carry" as a fund.

Many years later, once we earned that additional $9 million in returns from subsequent exits from the portfolio, we returned all our investor's capital in the form of cash, and the fund started to earn carry—yay! But how much of that carry money did *I* get to take home? To determine that amount, let's take a step back and talk about compensation at venture funds as a whole.

Whether you are investing out of your own pocket, you start a fund, or you join a fund, your personal compensation is structured in two pieces: salary and carry. Salaries come from the management fees, which means they are largely correlated to fund size. While big managers at big funds can make upwards of $1,000,000 per year in salary, if you are just starting out in the industry or running a small fund, your salary is likely not going to transform your life. As I interviewed other experienced investors for this book, I heard over and over again how one of the biggest misconceptions about venture capital is that it is lucrative from day one or that it is a glamorous job. As Danielle Strachman of 1517 Fund told me, "The first few years of our fund, we were making $50,000 a year, but we were okay with it because we knew that if we waited long enough for our companies to exit, the carry was where we were going to make our real money." This was a topic we had commonly commiserated upon, as I had a similar experience, barely scraping by on my salary at Fresco Capital in the expensive Bay Area before starting to see some returns flow back in the form of carry. In those early days, it was easy to project an image of being a big shot venture capitalist, but the truth was that my salary was lower than what most executive assistants and hair stylists in San Francisco earned on a yearly basis. I was just banking on the fact that my "carry stake," my personal share of the carry, would make up for it in the long run. This portion of compensation is very similar to an equity stake in a company—it represented my percentage share of the profits or my **ownership** in the fund.

Because carry stakes are calculated as an individual's percentage share of the 20 percent of the fund's share of the carried interest, it can be confusing to benchmark how much money flows back to you in the event of an exit after a fund has returned 1x (see Figure 5.1 for an example). The dollar amount of your carry also varies widely depending on the size of the fund, so the industry standard is to convert carry percentage into dollars if the fund returned 2x. This allows you to compare apples to apples when it comes to potential compensation. On my first $10 million fund, I thought I had hit it big because I had a 25 percent carry stake. That meant if we doubled the fund to $20 million, the first $10 million would go directly to repay limited partners for their initial capital invested. For the next $10 million in returns, 80 percent or $8 million would go back to limited partners and 20 percent or $2 million would go to the

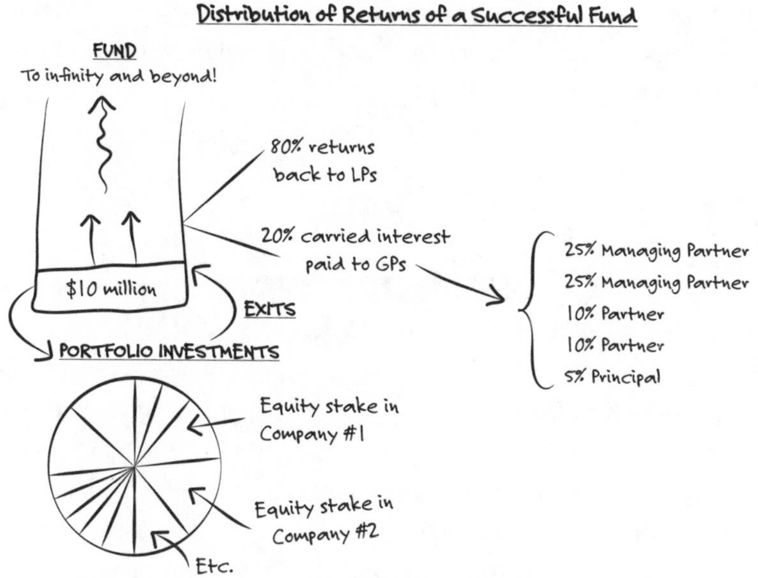

Distribution of Returns of a Successful Fund

Figure 5.1   If $10 million is invested in a portfolio of companies, the first $10 million of returns goes back to its LPs. Any additional profits are split first between LPs and the GP, then among the members of the GP according to their respective carry splits.

general partner as carried interest. My 25 percent cut of the $2 million would be $500,000.

By contrast, when I joined Trinity Ventures, my carry stake was 1 percent, which seemed like a dramatic step down in ownership from what I had been earning previously. However, Trinity's fund was roughly $400 million, much larger than that of Fresco. So, if we doubled the fund to $800 million, the first $400 million would go to directly repay limited partners for their initial capital invested. Then, of the next $400 million in returns, 80 percent or $320 million would go back to limited partners. The remaining 20 percent, roughly $80 million, would go to the general partner as carried interest.

There are plenty of considerations when deciding to start or join a fund, or how to negotiate or structure your compensation once you are there. Regardless of where you end up, it is important to make sure you know when, in what form, and how much of the returns will flow back to you personally in the case of an exit. This can and should play a significant role in how you think about making career decisions as well as investment decisions.

STEP 2

UNDERSTAND WHY
OWNERSHIP DRIVES RETURNS

Let's go back to Danielle's experience starting 1517 Fund. She was motivated to start investing in companies, instead of simply providing grants as a nonprofit, after she realized that she was leaving both money and influence on the table. How much you own of a business determines your ultimate payout at the time of an exit, but it also determines how much say you have in how things get done in the meantime. In both cases, your ownership percentage drives your returns.

In its simplest form, ownership percentage is calculated as your *capital invested* divided by your *post-money* valuation. In other words, at the time of an exit, your ownership percentage is the percentage of the profits to which you are entitled. Although it can be easy to focus simply on the number of dollars you are putting into a company, the percentage ownership you are acquiring as a result is actually more important as it will drastically impact your payout in the future.

For example, let's say you invest $100,000 into two startups. One has a $10 million post-money valuation, and the other has a $50 million post-money valuation. Both companies end up selling for $100,000,000. You put the same amount of money in, and the exit valuation is the same. Do you make the same amount in each transaction? Bear with me while we do the math.

Company #1: $100,000 invested

$10,000,000 post-money valuation = 1% ownership
At exit, 1% × $100,000,000 = **$1,000,000** in returns

Company #2: $100,000 invested

$50,000,000 post-money valuation = 0.2% ownership
At exit, 0.2% × $100,000,000 = **$200,000** in returns

That is a big difference in returns! While there are many different factors that go into the valuation of a startup, it is important to keep in mind that your *ownership percentage*—not just the dollars you invest and not the exit valuation—is what determines how much money you will make in the long run. Therefore, many large venture firms have *ownership targets* that they must acquire when making an investment. Ultimately, they care more about ownership than check size itself, because they know that ownership drives returns for both the fund and for themselves.

Not only does higher ownership mean more dollars back at the time of a liquidity event, but it also means you have more power over the path that a company takes to get there.

When I asked Kyle Lui about when he first learned the importance of ownership in venture capital, he recalled an early experience in his career at DCM Ventures when he learned that headline valuations at exits aren't the most important piece of the puzzle of making money in venture capital. He was an investor in a company called BitTorrent, a popular software company that allowed peer-to-peer file sharing, supporting users to distribute data and electronic files over the internet in a decentralized way. After a challenging few years, the company was sold for $140 million[1] to a blockchain startup called the Tron Foundation. In an industry that glorifies billion-dollar exits, the venture capital community largely regarded the exit as a failure. Kyle recalled to me, "It wasn't an impressive headline exit, but we owned 70 percent of the company at the time of the transaction, so it was actually huge for us in terms of returns." Indeed, the firm's 70 percent ownership stake minted them roughly $100,000,000 on the exit.

Not only does higher ownership mean more dollars back at the time of a liquidity event, but it also means you have more power over the path that a company takes to get there. This happens formally, as the largest shareholders in a company are often also members of the board of directors, but also informally as influential stakeholders tend to have a heavier hand in making big decisions about the future fate of the company. For example, looking back on my conversations with Kyle about BitTorrent, he specifically said, "We owned a majority of the company and played a big role in helping them move into crypto, which was a primary strategic decision that led to their acquisition." He described the process of exiting as "*We* sold the company." Clearly, Kyle was not a bystander in the process. Instead, as an investor with a significant ownership stake and a board seat, he was in the driver's seat.

Kyle's experience is very similar to what we learned in Principle 2 from Sarah Smith's early days at Bain Capital, when she was ultimately unable to invest in her friend's company, even though the CEO had verbally accepted her offer. The board of directors, made up of the investors with the largest ownership stakes in the business, had the final say. The experience underlined the importance of understanding how to read the air, but it also drives home the fact that increasing your ownership in a company gives you the opportunity to be on the other side of that equation—more ownership means you can be the one calling the shots.

Ownership can also play a significant role in your ability to *access* new opportunities in the future. As we discussed in Part One, winning access to high-quality deals requires a strong brand and reputation. Both entrepreneurs and potential limited partners in your funds are most interested in working with VCs that they believe can increase the odds of a successful outcome of an investment. Realistically, you can only influence the trajectory of a business if you have enough ownership to influence how decisions get made. That means more ownership now tends to lead to more ownership in the future as well.

I learned this firsthand when I was raising my first fund at Fresco Capital. Many early limited partners I pitched would say, "We want to see returns from your early investments before we feel comfortable investing in your fund." After I had two or three companies that sold at valuations far higher than when I invested, I went back to update them on my progress as a portfolio manager. I expected them to be thrilled! Unfortunately, instead of eagerly validating my talent as an investor, they asked, "Great, but how much did you own of each of those companies? What role did you play in helping them get acquired?"

In each case, I owned less than 2 percent of the company when it was acquired, which meant that I didn't have enough influence to be able to say what Kyle Lui did when he was talking about BitTorrent, "*We* sold the company."

As one investor told me directly, influencing outcomes through ownership was the difference between *betting* on great companies and *building* great companies. Truly building alongside an entrepreneur as their venture capitalist requires ownership, power, and influence.

STEP 3

AVOID TWO KEY PITFALLS WHEN NEGOTIATING OWNERSHIP

For the most part, based on what we've discussed so far, you are probably thinking that the more ownership you have in a company, the more likely you are to earn an impressive return on your investment. However, that would be far too simple! The reality of the relationship between ownership and returns is slightly more complicated. This is a result of two key concepts that most new investors tend to miss when it comes to negotiating ownership and analyzing how and when you will get money back from your investments: *dilution* and *founder ownership*. Both have a significant, and not necessarily intuitive, impact on the potential outcome of an investment. Therefore, it's critical to make sure you are at least aware of them when deciding how, when, and if to invest in a given opportunity.

First, let's talk about dilution. The math we did in Step 2 earlier demonstrated the importance of your ownership stake in a company; however, we left out one key detail—your ownership stake is very likely to change over time. In fact, the more money a company raises before it exits, the smaller your ownership stake will become. This is because every time a company raises money, it must issue new shares to sell to the new investors. This means that as an existing shareholder, you own the same number of shares, but the total number of shares goes up.

$$\text{Ownership \%} = \frac{\text{\# of shares you own}}{\text{Total \# shares}} = \frac{\text{\$ you invested}}{\text{Post-money valuation}}$$

Therefore, if the total number of shares goes up but your number of shares stays constant, your ownership goes down. This corresponding decrease in ownership is known as *dilution*.

For example, let's take a hypothetical investment I made in a future of work startup we'll call Company M. Company M enables teams to create "working agreements" that specify when, how, and where they will collaborate with each other. My investment thesis is that for remote and distributed teams, taking the implicit cooperation that used to happen in an office and making it concrete is critical to the long-term success of the company culture and, ultimately, the business. The company has a limited prototype that is early, but impressive, and the two cofounders have spent years working with large corporations coaching them on how to implement this type of process. Although they don't have any revenue yet, I decide to invest $2.5 million as the lead investor of a seed round at a $10 million post-money valuation. My $2.5 million invested earns me an ownership stake of 25 percent.

About a year later, Company M has built a working product, has thousands of very happy customers using it, and is approaching $1 million in annual recurring revenue. The cofounders decide to raise a Series A round from two new investors—VC #2 and VC #3—who each invest $5 million for a total of $10 million at a $30 million post-money valuation (Figure 5.2). Is this a good thing or a bad thing for me as an early investor? On one hand, my ownership will be lower. However, the company is valued at a higher dollar amount, so my shares are worth more. Let's see how it plays out (Table 5.1).

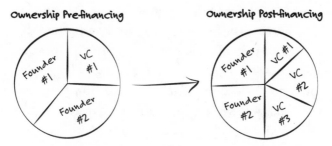

Figure 5.2 Ownership before and after new financing

First, let's look at what happens to my ownership.

$$\text{Dilution \%} = \frac{\text{\# of new shares issued}}{\text{New total share count}} = \frac{\text{\$ raised in new financing}}{\text{New post-money valuation}}$$

Table 5.1 Ownership before and after new financing

	Shares	Ownership	Shares Post-Financing	Ownership Post-Financing
Founder 1	375	37.5%	375	25%
Founder 2	375	37.5%	375	25%
VC 1	250	25%	250	16.7%
VC 2	0	0	250	16.7%
VC 3	0	0	250	16.7%
Total	1,000	100%	1,500	100%

In this case:

$$\text{Dilution \%} = \frac{500}{1,500} = \frac{\$10 \text{ million}}{\$30 \text{ million}} = 33.3\% \text{ dilution}$$

More specifically, my ownership stake of 25 percent is diluted by 33.3 percent and is now 16.7 percent.

My new ownership stake of 16.7 percent is lower than when I initially invested, which is not great, but I now own shares in a more valuable company. In fact, my initial investment of $2.5 million is now worth $5 million, or the equivalent of 16.7 percent of $30 million post-money. Moreover, the company has more cash on its balance sheet, which makes it possible to grow faster, hire more employees, and launch new initiatives that will increase its likelihood of future success.

So, you can see that raising additional capital at higher valuations is a double-edged sword. It reduces ownership but increases the likelihood of an exit occurring in the future at a higher valuation. There is no perfect answer to how much dilution is favorable versus unfavorable, as every situation is different, but it is a dynamic that you should be aware of when you are making an investment and thinking about your ownership over time. Be sure to consider—how much money is this company likely to raise before they exit? How will that impact my ownership and my eventual payout?

Many investors employ the strategy of *reserving follow-on capital* for their most successful investments. In other words, I would invest $2.5 million into Company M's seed round, but I would also set aside an additional $2.5 million to invest in the next round to buy additional shares and maintain my ownership percentage despite dilution. This strategy increases your potential payout at the time of an exit, since you own more of the company than if you had just accepted the dilution, but it also creates more risk since you are putting more money into a single investment that may or may not prove to be successful in the long run. The best thing you can do is analyze each round of investment as if it were a new company, using the process we discussed in Principle 4. Even though it is the same company you are investing in, how do the *current* team, technology, TAM, timing, and terms stack up? We'll discuss more in Principle 6 about how to avoid falling victim to some key biases when making decisions around follow-on investments.

In addition to taking on dilution from additional rounds of funding, there is one other scenario to consider where having *less* ownership in a company may actually be a *good* thing. That is when you are considering *ownership of founders and key executives*. As you can see from the example with Company M, founders of a company also take on dilution when they raise additional capital. Just like I learned when I was at Goldman Sachs, as mission driven as a founding team may be, they also want to make money. In fact, making money is a major motivating factor for most entrepreneurs! Many of the richest people in the world in 2022 are technology entrepreneurs who raised venture capital, including Jeff Bezos, the founder of Amazon; Larry Page, the cofounder of Google; and Elon Musk, the cofounder of SpaceX and CEO of Tesla. This type of wealth is the standard for success in entrepreneurship, and it must be within the realm of possibility in order to keep a team motivated to continue to do the very hard work, put in the long hours, and navigate the complex challenges involved in building a billion-dollar company.

You can expect that just as you are learning to calculate your potential payout at the time of an exit, smart founders and executives do the exact same thing. If the company raises too much money or takes on funding at a low valuation that is overly dilutive, then the team is likely to lose motivation to continue working hard. They may instead be incentivized to take a small or early exit opportunity so that they can collect some money and move on to their next opportunity. Therefore, in addition to optimizing your ownership stake, it is also important to consider how much ownership the team has after a financing. Although there is no hard-and-fast rule, and each individual has their own tolerance for risk/reward ratios, I typically get concerned about a founder or CEO owning less than 10 percent of their company. Even if it means reducing my ownership stake, I prefer that the leadership at the helm of the business is properly motivated to keep going when the times get tough, which they inevitably will.

I learned this the hard way through my investment in what I'll call Company B, a startup building software to make it easier for international students to apply to US colleges. When I first met Lily, the founder and CEO of Company B, I knew I wanted to invest in her. We were sitting in a gray conference room with no windows, but she lit up the room with her passion and articulate explanation of how this simple tool would remove barriers to high-quality secondary education and enable aspiring college graduates to find the best fit educational pathway for their goals, avoiding unnecessary stress and financial hardship in the process. She was raising a seed round of financing from a brand-name venture capital fund I'll call O Ventures. The firm was known for their smart investments and aggressive terms, meaning they liked to maximize their ownership in a company by whatever means possible. This case was no different as they were leading a $5 million round at a $10 million post-money valuation, resulting in 50 percent dilution for the existing founding team and angel investors.

> Even if it means reducing my ownership stake, I prefer that the leadership at the helm of the business is properly motivated to keep going when the times get tough, which they inevitably will.

As a follow-on investor, I was investing at the same terms set by O Ventures as a lead investor. I was initially happy with the relatively low valuation because it meant I could attain meaningful ownership even as a small investor, but I would soon learn the pitfalls of overly diluting a founding team. After the financing closed, the team got back to building the business, and they were able to grow significantly over the next four years. They raised two additional rounds of financing, and pretty soon Lily found that she owned only 7 percent of the company that she had started only a few years before.

As an early investor, I truly believed there were still exciting times ahead in this business that had a very impressive technology product, a world-class team, a large TAM, and a quickly changing higher education landscape that could result in perfect timing. However, the company was regularly getting inbound acquisition interest from larger, more traditional companies that wanted to buy their technology and customer base for future growth opportunities. Lily started to do the math on how much work she'd have to do to get Company B to be worth enough that her 7 percent stake would result in life-changing wealth for her and her family, and it started to look like a very long road ahead. She started to entertain the possibility of getting acquired, even if it was at a relatively low valuation.

Finally, she came to an agreement with a large company that expressed their intent to acquire her business for roughly $20 million. Just as the paperwork was starting to get finalized, news of a mysterious virus in China started to cast a gloom over financial markets and the stock market entered a free fall. The acquiring company cut their offer in half, and Lily accepted it. As an early investor who had spent years working alongside Lily to help build and expand the business, we were getting only a fraction of the money we had initially invested back. I couldn't help but believe Lily would have fought harder for a different outcome if she had stood to gain more from the transaction. Founder and key executive ownership is an important consideration when analyzing any potential investment.

Understanding how these key ingredients interact—money, ownership, power, and influence—is critical not only in earning a return on your investments in venture capital, but also in achieving change at scale.

At the end of the day, venture capital is so exciting because it is all about investing in changing the world at scale. In my experience, there is nothing more thrilling than spending my days at the intersection of technology and entrepreneurship, rubbing shoulders with people shaping the world of tomorrow. Many days, I tell myself that I would do this job even if I didn't get paid. I'd love to believe that, but then I remember my conversation with Pat in those early days on Wall Street and the fact that money matters. In venture capital, making money is driven by gaining ownership, and ownership goes hand in hand with power and influence. Understanding how these key ingredients interact—money, ownership, power, and influence—is critical not only in earning a return on your investments in venture capital, but also in achieving change at scale.

BREAKTHROUGH TIPS FOR MAKING MONEY MATTER IN VENTURE CAPITAL

- Be honest about your own motivations, as well as the motivations of others. Venture capital investing is ultimately driven by returns, and making money is a key incentive that will drive behavior over time.

- Remember that you won't make any money until you get cash back from your investments and you return all initial capital to your limited partners, which can take 5 to 10 years.

- Your ownership stake in a business determines how much control you have over the trajectory of the business, how much money you make off an exit, and how much credit you get for being an investor in that company.

- Dilution from additional rounds of funding will reduce your ownership stake, but also increase the odds of success of your investment. Consider the pros and cons carefully.

- Make sure that founders have the right amount of ownership so that your incentives are aligned, even if it means reducing your own ownership.

ACTIVELY MANAGE YOUR BLIND SPOTS

We have talked about analyzing investment opportunities by collecting data points about the people involved, the business being built, the market being transformed, and the potential payouts down the road. If you run a thorough due diligence process and you carefully weigh the risk and upside of a given investment, you are far more likely to make good investment decisions. However, there is one more key factor that you need to consider—*you*. As I look back on more than a decade of venture investments, there were certainly times when I passed on huge successes for good reasons—they didn't fit into my investment thesis, or I was worried there would be too much dilution before they exited. Or perhaps I made an investment believing that the market timing would work out, and it didn't play out that way.

On the other hand, there are quite a few companies I did or did not invest in because I misread or misinterpreted pieces of information due to my own personal biases. In my postmortem assessment of the investment, I realized that although I had collected the valuable information necessary to make a good decision, I had significant blind spots preventing me from properly analyzing the data points in front of me. In a world where you only hear or read about the massive successes, a phenomenon known as *survivorship bias*, I'll share with you some of the biggest mistakes I've made in hopes that you will learn to avoid the same pitfalls when making your investment decisions. By taking action during your diligence process toward recognizing these common forms of bias, you can and will become a better decision maker, and in turn, a more successful venture capitalist. As Ice Cube wisely stated, "Check yo'self before you wreck yo'self."

1. Take stock of personal emotional biases.

2. Validate claims that sound too good to be true.

3. Confirm that the founder's vision is aligned with yours.

4. Evaluate every follow-on investment as if it were a new investment.

STEP 1

TAKE STOCK OF PERSONAL EMOTIONAL BIASES

It is not controversial to state that there is not much diversity in technology, entrepreneurship, and venture capital. In 2020, female-led startups attracted 2.3 percent of total venture capital dollars.[1] Similarly, between 2015 and 2020, Black and Latinx–led companies commanded 2.6 percent of total venture capital funding raised during that time.[2] Although 40 percent of venture capital firms claim to have diversity, equity, and inclusion programs in place, it still appears that very little has changed in terms of the types of founders attracting funding.[3] This is probably because 93 percent of venture capital dollars are still controlled by white men, according to a 2019 study by the James L. Knight Foundation.[4]

In my early days as a venture capitalist, before the #metoo movement brought much-needed awareness to the overarching rhetoric about women in business, this glaring gender imbalance in venture meant I was constantly flooded by both subtle and not-so-subtle negative messages about my capability as an investor due to my being female. I once flew from Tokyo to New York for 24 hours to meet the Dubai-based patriarch of what I will call the Vikas family, a group that had made billions building a large network of private schools. They had invested in several venture capital funds I knew, and they were particularly interested in getting access to more investment opportunities in education technology, which was my primary focus area at the time. We had already coinvested in several companies, which is usually a strong indication of alignment. In every way, it seemed like a perfect fit, so I seized the opportunity to put an end to years of pitching their team on why they should invest and finally make my case to the real decision maker—the father of the family whom I will call Arun.

I was initially introduced to the Vikas family through one of their technology advisors who had spent hours "picking my brain" on the market and asking for introductions to my network. When he realized I might stop being so helpful if he couldn't provide any value in return, he offered to set up the meeting with Arun so I could pitch him on investing in my fund. However, he also warned me that Arun was "very traditional" and it "might be a good idea for me to invite one of my male partners for the meeting as well."

Although I was somewhat miffed by the idea of going into business with someone who held this type of viewpoint, I was more interested in getting the deal done, so I obliged and invited my partner Steve to join us in New York for the meeting. He was all set to fly in and meet Arun along with me, but in a fateful twist of irony, an epic winter snowstorm caused his flight to be cancelled, without any hope of rescheduling for several days. Airports were shut down and nothing was getting in or out of New York. Except, apparently, for international flights, because my flight from Tokyo took off on time without incident and was one of the only flights to get into the city that day. I had no choice but to face the meeting solo.

Once in New York, after an anxious and jet-lagged night of sleep, I rode the subway up to the Four Seasons Hotel, where I was instructed to wait in the lobby for a text message that would reveal the room number where our meeting would take place. It was fitting that the hotel was situated on what is known as Billionaire's Row, and I felt a rush of adrenaline as I walked through the impressive front entrance and heard the heels of my black boots click against the perfectly polished marble floors. I stood nervously near the front desk, taking in the tasteful yet ornate decorations of the five-star accommodations and awaiting this mysterious text message from the team handling the all-powerful Arun.

Fifteen minutes of suspense later, my phone finally pinged with the promised instructions, and I rode up the shiny elevator, wondering what this meeting would have in store for me. As I opened the heavy front door to the suite, Arun was standing on the other side of the entryway, furiously tapping away on his cell phone in what appeared to be a Juicy Couture–like velour jumpsuit. He had the air of someone who wanted you to think he didn't care about anything, but clearly cared a lot about sending you that message.

Alarmed by the sound of the heavy door closing behind me, his thumbs paused from his message just long enough to look up at me and ask, "I'm sorry, who are you?" I nervously explained that I was Allison, and that his advisor had invited me here to talk about my venture capital fund, Fresco Capital. Clearly surprised, he finally put his phone down to his side, looked directly at me incredulously, and said, "*You?* Run a venture capital fund?"

Any semblance of confidence I had mustered on the way over was immediately shattered by his lack of knowledge of our meeting and apparent disbelief of my role as a venture capitalist. At a loss for a snappy response, I mustered a weak, "Yes, I mean, along with my partners . . ." and proceeded to stumble through several more hours of rapid-fire questions that appeared to have nothing to do with the topic of investing in education technology. I did my best to use every opportunity to demonstrate my market knowledge, network, and the early success in my portfolio, but Arun's continuous tapping on his phone and lack of interest in the substantive information one would need to make a decision about whether or not to invest in a venture capital fund made it obvious I was being dismissed. By the time 11:30 rolled around, I was grateful for a subtle knock at the door and the delivery of a lavish lunch spread along with a very expensive bottle of Chardonnay. After declining to drink, I was told I had no choice because this was "their tradition" and it "would be rude not to join them." I had never felt less powerful.

There were many cases where I skipped key diligence steps in objectively assessing a market opportunity because I was so driven by a deep sense of responsibility and obligation to be an advocate for female entrepreneurs.

Because I experienced this type of dismissal as a female founder of a venture capital fund, I have always deeply sympathized with female founders of companies. Even though I was raising capital for a fund, and they were raising money for companies, we were in the same trenches, fighting for respect, recognition, and resources. Of course, it was always refreshing and therapeutic to bond on a personal level and swap equally shocking yet commonplace stories about our experiences with male investors. Investing in female and underrepresented founders became a core part of my investment thesis. I believed that underrepresented entrepreneurs were systematically overlooked and underestimated and would outperform relative to their peers. By speaking and writing about this thesis wherever I could, my focus and dedication to female founders allowed me to streamline my deal flow and direct my network to make relevant introductions.

However, because this element of my thesis was deeply personal, there were many cases where I skipped key diligence steps in objectively assessing a market opportunity because I was so driven by a deep sense of responsibility and obligation to be an advocate for female entrepreneurs. This was the case with my investment in Company A, an education technology startup I backed early in my career as a VC. The business offered subscription kits for kids to help them learn about science, technology, engineering, and math. At the time, there was a cultural zeitgeist around the dramatic shift in jobs away from traditional sectors and toward technology jobs. There was an emerging crisis around the shortage of engineers, and parents and educators alike were becoming concerned that kids in grade school today were learning skills for jobs that likely wouldn't exist by the time they entered the labor force. The government was unlocking big budgets for STEM education tools, and parents were clamoring for innovative ways to get their kids excited about learning technology. Sarah, the CEO of Company A, had experience as an early employee at another education startup, and she was passionate about the mission of democratizing access to technology skills from an early age. I started checking the boxes in my diligence process around founder/market fit, unique technology, a large TAM, and early ingredients for optimal market timing.

As the investment round came together and we started learning more about the potential terms being offered by lead investors, however, I couldn't help but notice the valuation was far lower than what I had expected. On one hand, I was intrigued by the potential to buy a strong ownership stake early on, but the terms seemed too good to be true. Over coffee, Sarah revealed that she believed she was being significantly underestimated because she was a female CEO. She asked me to meet with the lead investor she was talking to in order to find out whether he had legitimate questions about the business or he simply didn't believe she was capable because he was biased against women. Having been in so many similar situations myself, I could already feel my blood boiling with a sense of injustice.

Intensely motivated by my desire to support a female founder who was likely being undervalued, I cleared my schedule to do a reference call with the investor in question. His endless line of questions about her experience and whether or not she knew how to build a business confirmed my suspicion that he was biased against her, focusing on his perception of her potential as a CEO instead of the massive market opportunity at hand. I did my best to assert my views about the technology, TAM, and timing, but he was unconvinced. He viewed her as a risky investment and had made up his mind that his best offer to invest would be at a very low valuation where he could own a significant amount of the company and maintain decision-making control in case Sarah was not able to perform as CEO. After hanging up, I called Sarah to let her know that I agreed with her assessment that he was biased against her. In an emotional decision, I told her that in order to avoid wasting any more time with male investors who were likely to come to the same conclusion, I would lead the round instead.

At this point, I had stopped digging deeper on the diligence side because I had already made up my mind. However, after we made the investment and we started having our first board meetings, I realized there were major red flags. The subscription kits had missed important manufacturing deadlines, and the company had still not seen any sales materialize. There was significant turnover among early employees, and there was a lack of clear direction when it came to sales and product strategy. These challenges ultimately became too much to overcome, and the company shut down several years later. In my postmortem analysis, I realized that my personal biases had prevented me from completing an objectively sound analysis about the potential of the business.

It's not just me, either—everyone has some lived experience that could drive them to make emotionally biased investment decisions. One person I know was devastated by his wife's breast cancer diagnosis, and shortly afterward got so excited about a company using AI to detect breast cancer early that he didn't ask the hard questions he needed to in order to properly analyze the business opportunity. Another friend of mine whose kids struggled to get into college invested in better test prep software without considering the competitive landscape that could prevent the company from growing quickly enough to justify venture capital funding. The chances to make emotional, one-dimensional choices are endless. The only antidote to our biases, triggers, and blind spots is self-awareness.

Here is how I recommend taking stock of your emotional biases:

- **Create a checklist for your diligence process and key questions you need to ask every entrepreneur before making an investment decision.** No matter how strongly you feel about an investment, ensure you have answers to each question before you proceed. Keep a record and review it regularly during your postmortems.

- **Incorporate people with diverse perspectives into your decision-making process.** Whether they are your investment partners, friends, or trusted advisors, check your reasoning with someone who has lived life differently from you. Does your logic make sense to them as well? If it doesn't, you might be over-indexing based on your personal experience.

- **Bring awareness to the role your emotions are playing in your decisions by taking stock of how personally you are taking this investment.** How would you feel if you walked away from this opportunity? If you took a personal event or experience out of the equation, would this innovation still appeal to you? How would you feel if this company failed? If you would take these outcomes personally, you might be losing a sense of objectivity.

STEP 2

VALIDATE CLAIMS THAT SOUND TOO GOOD TO BE TRUE

Sitting on a sun-drenched bench outside the Ferry Building in San Francisco, it was easy to get swept up by the excitement of a founder I will call Evan, who had a grand vision for creating a social network for charitable causes. For privacy purposes, I'll call the company Stance.

The crisp air blew in off the Bay, slightly chilling my hands as they clutched a perfectly warm Blue Bottle almond milk latte. I tried to draw my attention to the physical sensation amid a very heady conversation about changing the world at scale. I had set up a meeting with Evan on one of my regular trips to Silicon Valley from Japan at the urging of my partner, who had already met Evan through a mutual friend and had been impressed by his vision. My partner thought we should consider investing in the company, even though it had not yet been built.

It was clear that Evan was an experienced entrepreneur driven by his passion for making social impact go mainstream. He wanted to leverage the millennial enthusiasm for changing the world to build a new social network exclusively focused on raising money for nonprofits. His new app had an A-list roster of advisors and angel investors, most notably Biz Stone, the cofounder of Twitter. Evan told me that Biz was heavily involved in the app development. He recounted how he had met Biz over dinner, and after he explained what he was building, Biz had been completely blown away by how visionary the concept was—he said that this was exactly what he *wished* Twitter had become and immediately offered to invest money and also to become a close advisor on the product development. Given the massive success of Twitter, it was hard to deny that Biz's endorsement was powerful and that his personal involvement could make a big difference in the ultimate success of Stance.

As a relative newcomer to Silicon Valley, I was impressed by the endorsement of such a technology celebrity, and I expressed my eagerness to connect with him myself and hear more about why he chose to back Stance. As I finished my latte, Evan assured me that *of course* he could introduce us, but Biz was very busy and he needed to figure out the right time. The only issue, he told me, was that now that Biz was involved, lots of investors were eager to put money into Stance as well, and the seed round was coming together very quickly, so we would need to make a decision swiftly. Although Evan did connect us with Biz over email, Biz never responded. I continued to push to verify his point of view on the business, but my emails remained unanswered.

Meanwhile, Evan kept reminding us that there was a lot of competition from others to invest, and if we wanted to participate in the round, we had to decide quickly. He emphasized that he was carefully considering whose money he would take, and there was a long list of other A-listers who wanted to invest, including billionaire cofounder of PayPal Peter Thiel, Salesforce CEO Marc Benioff, and famed venture capitalist Marc Andreessen. Normally, existing investors in startups are very willing to hop on a phone with another prospective investor to share their thoughts and reasoning for investing. As we learned in earlier chapters, these reference calls are critical to deals getting done. As a result, I was a bit skeptical about Biz Stone's level of involvement given that he apparently wasn't interested in serving as a reference for Evan. That fact, plus the rush to decide, gave me a lingering "Spidey-Sense" that something wasn't right.

On the other hand, I figured that as a famed cofounder of Twitter, Biz must be very busy, and maybe he didn't check his emails in the same way regular people did. Plus, if there were so many other technology celebrities vying for allocation in the round, there must be something exciting behind Evan and his vision for Stance. So we decided to go ahead and invest.

Name-dropping can be a very manipulative way to invoke social proof bias.

After we made the investment, it started to become clear that neither Biz Stone nor any of the other big names that Evan had been dropping were involved in the day-to-day operations of building Stance. In fact, when we inquired about the final ownership allocations after the round closed, Evan told us that many of these celebrities "didn't make it into the round" at all. I was beginning to suspect they were never around the table in the first place. What else became clear was that Evan was wholly incapable of translating his big vision into any kind of real product. He was great at telling stories, but there was absolutely no follow-through. In fact, it was less than a year after that fated almond milk latte that the company ran out of money and shut down completely.

Reflecting further on how my own bias had hindered clear analysis of the opportunity at hand, I realized I had fallen subject to "social proof bias." **Social proof** is a cognitive bias that occurs when you believe and trust that other people know something better than you do. When used with the intention to deceive, name dropping can be a very manipulative way to invoke social proof bias. It is exceedingly unattractive in personal settings but very easy to fall for in professional ones, especially in the opaque world of venture capital when it is nearly impossible to verify some of the claims that entrepreneurs make during the fundraising process. Even if famous names are involved in a startup, it's impossible to know why unless you take the time and effort to verify the claim. Perhaps they were pressured by a friend or owed someone a favor. Or it's not even them personally who is involved, but someone from their staff. Perhaps they're building a portfolio and this individual investment or project means very little to them. Maybe they didn't even invest money but just agreed to lend their name as an advisor.

At the end of the day, the best person to make an investment decision for your portfolio is *you*, regardless of who else is supposedly involved. Take the necessary time and steps to validate claims from entrepreneurs and assess the viability of an investment opportunity given your own goals and portfolio strategy.

Here are methods for validating claims that sound too good to be true:

- **Do not let an entrepreneur rush you into making a decision without completing your full diligence process.** Even if there is a short timeline, the right founders or CEOs will work nights and weekends alongside you to help get the information as quickly as possible so you can make a decision with conviction.

- **Connect in person or on a video call with any influential advisors, team members, or investors you see as critical to the competitive advantage of the company you are investing in.** Verify their motivations, their aspirations for the business, and their level of involvement.

- **During CEO references, inquire about their track record for honesty and ethics.** Has there ever been a situation where they have not been transparent or up front with their colleagues, friends, or collaborators?

STEP 3

CONFIRM THAT THE FOUNDER'S VISION IS ALIGNED WITH YOURS

Whether it's taking a new job, starting a new relationship, or investing in a new company, starting any risky venture requires a special cocktail of confidence, optimism, and naivete. After all, taking on a new challenge would be overly daunting if you weren't able to visualize what an ideal outcome could be. As an investor, focusing on the unlimited potential of our ownership stakes generates adrenaline and excitement and helps drown out all the endless reasons why companies fail. If we didn't get pumped up about every one of our portfolio companies, we wouldn't do this job! Early in my career as an investor, when I was considering an investment, I would literally write out a potential headline announcing the company's successful outcome. Did it seem feasible? Would I be proud to read it? Not exactly the most scientific process, but at the time, it helped me generate the courage I needed to swing for the fences.

While this process of envisioning the ultimate success can play an important role in a decision-making process, it can also lead to an inflated sense of importance when it comes to determining the eventual shape of a business. Even if you have a meaningful ownership stake, many venture capitalists forget that they are not the ones actually building these companies. Almost every venture capital firm's website may assert that they are "rolling their sleeves up and build alongside founders," but investors don't build world-changing companies. Founders do.

In the midst of falling in love with a company's potential to change the world, it can be all too easy to end up investing in *your* vision as an investor, and not in the founder's vision as the primary builder of the company. When these two visions are not aligned, it can lead to some harsh surprises down the road. I call this bias in the decision making process "projecting your vision," but it is commonly known as a form of **confirmation bias**, which is when you have already made up your mind and you are merely searching for evidence to prove you are right.

> Investors don't build world-changing
> companies. Founders do.

During my interview with Jomayra Herrera, general partner at education-focused venture capital firm Reach Capital, we laughed as we recalled how many times we've each made this mistake. In fact, Jomayra shared that she believes she fell victim to confirmation bias when she was investing in the company that initially brought us together. Jomayra and I were first connected when I was doing my due diligence on a company I will call SES, Inc., a software system for hiring hourly workers in call centers. Their algorithms leveraged dozens of data points based on personality type, speed of learning, lifestyle, and other factors so they could better match hourly workers with jobs where they were likely to stay and succeed.

As part of my regular due diligence checklist, I requested an introduction to the investor leading the round. Early the next morning in Tokyo, I found myself on the phone with Jomayra, who was calling me on one of her sunny afternoon walks in Palo Alto, where she was based at the time. I introduced myself, provided context for my interest in connecting, and proceeded to ask a series of detailed questions about her decision to invest. I was impressed by how well she articulated the future vision of the business and agreed with her assessment of its massive potential to transform the lives of call center workers around the world.

As we recounted this phone call during our interview so many years later, I mentioned how impressed I had been with her analysis of the market opportunity. Jomayra chuckled at my compliment, then grew serious as she explained, "I was so academic and theoretical about what I believed would work and where I saw opportunity in that business. I had a 200-slide deck on the future of work and how I believed it was going to evolve over time. By the time I met the founders, I had already built a vision in my head of what this company could be and where it could grow over time. I completely disregarded spending more time with the team and understanding what they could actually build."

Several years later, when the company failed to produce any meaningful revenue and most of its founding team moved on to other endeavors, the business was sold for pennies on the dollar. All of the early investors, including Jomayra and myself, walked away with nothing. In her postmortem analysis, Jomayra identified that this was a classic case of confirmation bias, where she had made up her mind before she even started diligence, so she only sought out information that confirmed her existing belief that this was going to be a massively successful company.

"When you have a vision in your head," she told me, "you confirm your own biases with the information that comes in. Sure, I talked to customers, but I heard all the good and discounted all the bad. I definitely projected a vision. I don't think the founders even said they had that same vision, but I wasn't listening."

It is perfectly natural to have a gut feeling about a company or a founder and want very badly for that gut feeling to be true. Especially when you're investing in ideas that get you out of bed in the morning, it is essential to get excited about what is possible for a new business. However, invest the proper time and effort to make sure that your vision is aligned with that of the founder who is actually building the company.

Here are some ways to confirm that the founder's vision is aligned with yours:

- **Write down what your future vision is for a business.** This can be as simple as writing that "massive success" headline like I did, or drilling down into specifics around what a company would need to achieve to generate a meaningful outcome for your investment. What will the product need to do? How much revenue do they need to be making? How many customers will they need? Get concrete and specific; don't just create big vision statements. Do these numbers align with the projections outlined in the investment materials?

- **During your early meetings with companies, founders, coinvestors, and references, focus on framing your questions only in an open-ended manner.** Don't lead the witness! For example:

  Don't Ask: "If you IPOed for a billion dollars, would that feel like success for you?"
  Do Ask: "What does success look like for you?"

  Don't Ask: "Are you worried about how your costs might increase over time?"
  Do Ask: "What keeps you up at night?"

  Don't Ask: "Do you think you can go public if you hit $20 million in revenue?"
  Do Ask: "What milestones do you need to reach for an IPO?"

  Don't Ask: "They are incredible visionaries, aren't they?"
  Do Ask: "What are the company's biggest strengths?"

- **Ask one of your partners, friends, or close advisors to talk through the opportunity with you and play devil's advocate.** What would a skeptic say about this opportunity, and have you adequately addressed this hypothetical skeptic's concerns with data and research?

STEP 4

EVALUATE EVERY FOLLOW-ON INVESTMENT AS IF IT WERE A NEW INVESTMENT

Everyone loves an underdog story. The promise of a person, team, or company coming from behind and beating out the competition renews our faith in the universe and in our own resilience. This was certainly the case with Brian, the founder and CEO of one of my firm's investments in a company I will call Company W. Brian grew up in a working-class family. His father built an injury prevention consulting business, where he worked with truck drivers and delivery men and helped them complete physical therapy exercises that would prevent potential painful injuries that could ruin their livelihoods. Brian's father build a solid business, but he ultimately failed to scale it to the size that would be necessary to change their family's socioeconomic status.

After a tour on Wall Street, earning an Ivy League MBA, and performing some operational work at an early stage startup, Brian knew it was his destiny to help his father turn his business into the success that he always knew it could be. He hired some engineers and built a technology-driven version of his father's training program that allowed companies to purchase high-quality and effective training videos for workers to view online or on their mobile phones. By making this type of training easy and more accessible, Company W helped workers avoid injuries that would prevent them from working. Brian insisted they could also save companies millions of dollars per year by avoiding worker's compensation insurance payouts, as well as avoiding the cost of replacing workers temporarily if they became injured and couldn't work.

The company was able to generate early promising sales numbers, capturing the customer base of Brian's family business and making inroads into the new e-commerce driven supply chain. Most notably, they found their way into Amazon, which bought their solution for preventing injuries amongst their warehouse workers, who were notoriously on their feet for long hours fulfilling their millions of daily orders. While the product was compelling, the market size was very large, and there was evidence of customer demand, we were most excited by the momentum and the strong evidence of founder/market fit—the CEO had personal experience with the problem he was solving, a highly relevant existing network in the industry, and a personal passion for the mission of the business. In that sense, Brian had it all. My firm at the time decided to lead Brian's $8 million Series A for a 20 percent ownership stake and a board seat.

In the months and quarters after the investment, however, Brian was unable to continue the momentum of his early success. Even though he had some early revenue, his customers were not demonstrating that they would increase their contract sizes in the future. In fact, some of them **churned**, meaning they decided not to continue their contracts after they expired. Sales stalled. Our board meetings became tense as Brian spent most of the time providing a lengthy list of excuses why he had not gotten any new revenue in the last several months—contracts were delayed, decision makers were changing companies, it was the wrong time of year, they had an underperforming salesperson who was not doing their job well . . . the list went on and on. Slow months stretched into quarters, and ultimately a year went by with no new revenue at all. Things were not looking good.

Typical investment cycles in venture capital are 12 to 18 months, meaning companies will raise enough money to survive for 12 to 18 months before they need to raise additional capital to keep growing. At that point, they will either raise a follow-on round, shut down, or try to cut costs, become profitable, and position for a sale. Because

venture capital focuses on high-growth businesses that are not immediately profitable, but instead require up-front investment to develop
new technology or go-to-market strategies, investors pay close attention to something called **runway**. Similar to the distance that planes
have on the runway before they either stop or take off, runway is the
length of time that a company can continue to grow unprofitably
before it goes bankrupt. To put it extremely simply, if your business makes $300,000 per month and your total costs are $400,000
per month, your **burn rate**, or the amount of money you are losing
every month, is equal to $100,000. If you raise $1,000,000 in cash,
then you have 10 months of runway before you either go bankrupt,
raise more money, or become profitable. When deciding how much
money to raise, most investors and founders recommend 18 months
of runway. This seems like a reasonable amount of time to demonstrate growth and progress, while still creating a sense of urgency for
everyone involved.

As we discussed in Principle 5, maintaining ownership over time
is a key part of ensuring you make money from your investments.
That means that after you make an initial investment, you will need
to decide in each subsequent follow-on round of funding whether
or not you will invest more capital to maintain or even increase your
ownership. When things are going very well, it can seem like an obvious decision. However, when things are not working and a business is
not growing as quickly as it should, most entrepreneurs will tell you
that they just need more time. Of course, this directly translates to
more money.

When Brian's runway started to grow alarmingly short, he asked
us as his largest investors to provide him with more capital so he could
live to fight another day and fix whatever was preventing them from
growing faster. We had invested $6 million into the business thus
far, and it definitely felt as if the decision to invest additional capital boiled down to the choice between admitting certain defeat or
increasing our ownership and maintaining the possibility of a very
large outcome sometime in the future.

This decision point is often affected by a concept called **sunk cost fallacy,** which taps into your fear of losing what you have already invested. It is common not only in investing, but in any situation where you have spent time, money, effort, or emotions. Have you stayed in a relationship longer than you should have just because you've already invested so much in building a life with that person? Have you finished your entire plate of food even after you were full just because you paid for it already? These are all examples of this well-researched cognitive bias that leads us to believe that past decisions will affect future outcomes. In venture capital, especially if you have been mindful of how you have been investing your time, it is all too easy to forget that whatever you have invested previously actually has no influence on the ultimate outcome of a business.

> If a business is not working already, there
> is a reason why, and that reason is not
> that they don't have enough money.

Instead, it is important to consider every follow-on investment decision as if it were a new investment. Is the business working already? If you just met a founder and heard their pitch today, how would you evaluate the opportunity according to your regular diligence process? If a business is not working already, there is usually a reason why, and that reason is not usually that they don't have enough money. Perhaps the product is not what the market really wants or needs, or the team is not properly positioned to attack the opportunity. Most likely, the timing is not quite right and there are not sufficient tailwinds to support exponential growth in the term. None of these problems can be solved with additional capital.

In the case of Company W, we decided not to reinvest in the business, and neither did any of the other investors. Ultimately, Brian sold his business to a consulting firm, and we received no money back from our initial investment. Underdog stories make us feel good, but they are very rare in venture capital. Whether you are investing in a new opportunity or evaluating whether to add capital to an existing investment, it is important to separate yourself from your previous decisions and remember that you cannot recover the time, capital, and emotions you have already put into the opportunity. Take stock of how the business is performing today, and do not be afraid to cut your losses and move on when the situation warrants it.

Here's how to evaluate each follow-on investment as if it were a new investment:

- **Complete your full due diligence process—references, back channels, and all—for each round of funding that a company raises after your initial investment.**

- **Identify the key reasons outside of capital that are contributing to a company's momentum (or lack thereof).** Is it the technology itself? The timing? The competition? Are these factors within the control of the team with clear solutions, or are they open-ended challenges?

- **Carefully consider the other ways you could use that capital instead.** Are there other opportunities in your pipeline that you are evaluating at the same time? Challenge yourself to rank the follow-on opportunity versus other new investment opportunities. Which have better risk/reward?

HOW TO RUN A POSTMORTEM ANALYSIS OF YOUR INVESTMENT DECISIONS

It can take years, if not decades, for the ultimate fate of a startup to come to fruition. In many cases, you will be running "postmortems" 1, 2, or even up to 10 years after you completed your due diligence on an investment opportunity. By that time, you will probably have completed due diligence on countless other opportunities, which can make it difficult to accurately recall your decision-making process for the company in question. Therefore, the first step in running a good postmortem analysis is maintaining rigorous records from each time you analyze a potential investment opportunity. I always like to think I can remember how things went down, but am regularly surprised in my postmortems by the wedge that time and new experiences inevitably drive between my memory and the reality of my due diligence process.

Here are some key steps you can take for running a postmortem analysis of your investment decisions. If you apply this process, you will inevitably become a more skilled decision maker and a more successful venture capitalist.

1. First, create a reliable and searchable system for tracking your investment decisions. For each company you are considering investing in, be sure to log the following information:
   a. Source of introduction
   b. Company
   c. Date of evaluation
   d. Confirmed completion of your diligence checklist (whatever it may be)
   e. Your notes and a numerical assessment of each key diligence factor:
      i. Team
      ii. Technology
      iii. Terms
      iv. TAM
      v. Timing

    f.   Notes on key investment merits (what do you love) and key investment considerations (what do you not love so much)

    g.   Your investment decision—yes/no, amount

2. Set a regular cadence—I suggest twice per year—to review your investment decisions and the ultimate outcomes of the companies you were analyzing. Allow yourself at least 60 minutes, and invite anyone else who is part of your decision-making process (your partners, advisors, team members, etc.).

3. If you ended up investing, take stock of the following questions:

    a.   How much is your investment worth today? How much do you believe it will be worth in the future?

    b.   What were the risks you identified when you invested? Did these risks end up being significant factors in the growth trajectory of the business?

    c.   What were the key merits you identified when you invested? Did these factors end up being influential in the outcome of your investment?

    e.   Were there any assumptions you made that turned out not to be true?

    f.   Was there any key information that you missed?

    g.   Is there anything you could have done differently in your due diligence process that would have influenced your ultimate decision?

4. If you did not invest:

    a.   What is your best estimate for how much your investment would be worth today? If it would have been a big winner, then this company belongs in your anti-portfolio!

b. What were your primary reasons for not investing? Did the risks you identified turn out to be accurate?

c. Were there assumptions you made that turned out not to be true?

d. Was there any key information that you missed?

e. Is there anything you could have done different in your analysis process that would have influenced your ultimate decision?

5. In reviewing your answers for the previous questions, is there anything you can change about your process for analyzing investments that might lead to better or different outcomes?

6. Have you revealed any biases or blind spots that you need to adapt for in future investment decisions?

I must admit to you that as I have been writing this chapter, a thought has nagged me. In the process of outlining all the ways in which I have fallen victim to my own biases and blind spots, I couldn't help but think, *Oh my god, I am a terrible investor. Who am I to even be writing this book considering I have made so many poor investment decisions?* It is not uncommon to take a pause and question oneself, but sitting down to explain all the things you've done wrong over the years tends to really drive home the point.

However, I must remind myself, and you, that failure is a feature, not a bug, of venture capital. Just like a batter who can't possibly hit every ball out of the park, there are inevitably going to be a lot of swings and a lot of misses. A typical venture capital portfolio is designed for about one-third of your investments to go to zero. Another one-third should be average returns, and one-third or less will be home runs. In fact, true success requires hitting out of the park only a few times in your entire career. You cannot, and should not, be right 100 percent of the time. What is most important is that you keep swinging for the fences, which means taking risks and some-times getting them wrong.

At the end of the day, we are only human, and every invest-ment decision is an opportunity to become more skilled at your craft as a venture capitalist. Approach your mistakes with curiosity, not judgment. If you do, chances are you'll learn the most from the investments you made that didn't work because you'll learn about how to better analyze each opportunity in the future by actively man-aging your blind spots instead of letting them catch you off guard.

BREAKTHROUGH TIPS FOR ACTIVELY MANAGING YOUR BLINDSPOTS

- Do the work to cultivate self-awareness of how your past experiences and your current life contexts might influence your decision-making process.

- Surround yourself with people that are different from you, and regularly engage in conversations where you leverage their perspectives and insights.

- Remember that celebrity investors are not necessarily more knowledgeable than you are when it comes to thoroughly evaluating an investment opportunity. Just because people know their name, does not mean they have better judgment than you.

- Exercise discipline when it comes to completing your due diligence checklist on every investment, whether it is a new addition to your portfolio or a follow-on investment.

- Be kind to yourself when you are wrong. Remember that you are constantly learning and improving your process as you gain new information.

PART THREE

ADD VALUE

Several years ago, I met the founders of Company Y, a company building easy-to-use asynchronous video recordings—think Snapchat or TikTok—for the business world. For the first time, anyone could easily record a video, a screen share, or both, and share it just as quickly and intuitively as sharing a photo. In a quickly changing business world where teams were starting to collaborate remotely and asynchronously, the demand for this functionality was growing every day, and it showed in their numbers. The founders were young and energetic, their technology was incredibly unique, the potential TAM was huge, and their product traction was undeniable. Plus, the timing of the business world starting to adopt consumer-grade technology as young digital natives graduated into positions of power was an absolute no-brainer.

My partners and I were so excited to invest in their business that we wrote them an aggressive term sheet, valuing them at much higher levels than even the rest of our firm wanted to support, but we did it anyway with the belief that if we invested, this company could be worth a lot more money in a very short period of time. Unfortunately, we weren't the only ones who found the opportunity compelling, and the company had their choice of lead investors for the round. The other potential leads were just as aggressive on valuation, so it was hard to stand out on terms alone. Instead, the founders were asking tough questions like, "What else do you bring to the table that can help me grow faster? What do you have to offer besides just money?"

Although my firm at the time had a great reputation and we tried to lean on our shared values, storied history of successful investments, and deep network in the technology ecosystem in the Bay Area, these differentiators were simply not enough to win the deal. We were competing against several of the oldest and most well-regarded venture capital firms on Sand Hill Road. These firms had much larger funds than we did, including dedicated growth funds, so they promised the founders of Company Y that they would continue to invest as they grew, making future fundraising processes more efficient and less of a distraction. Additionally, they had specialized resources for adding value to their investments in the form of full teams of professionals with backgrounds in marketing, sales, and recruiting that Company Y could leverage to help scale up and supplement their existing team.

Not only did these competing firms have very specific ways in which they could add value beyond the round of funding itself, they also had complex sales processes for convincing the founders they were the right partner. These involved sending thoughtful and highly personal gifts to the entire Company Y executive team, formal sales pitches where they presented PowerPoint decks outlining their service offerings, and enlisting other founders they had worked with to reach out to the Company Y team to vouch for them. It hurt to lose, but if I was being honest with myself, I completely understood why they wouldn't choose us. We were simply outmatched.

Less than two years later, I wasn't surprised when I saw a headline announcing Company Y's new round of funding that valued them at $1.5 billion. A sense of overwhelming frustration washed over me as I officially added them to my anti-portfolio. We had known there was something special there, but we didn't get the chance to be part of it. What poured salt in the wound was that we didn't miss out because we didn't have access, nor was it because we didn't analyze the deal properly. It was simply because we didn't have enough of a strategy for *adding value*.

Indeed, seeing good deal flow is the beginning of the road. Selecting which ones to fight for is a big part of the journey. But winning the opportunity to invest in the ones you want to is what ultimately determines where you end up, and winning is all about how you add value. As we have discussed earlier in the book, the reality is that more than $200 billion in US dollars is invested in technology startups every year, yet the number of venture-backable businesses started every year has remained relatively constant. Consequently, capital is quickly becoming commoditized, and investing in the best opportunities is incredibly competitive. Figuring how to put yourself in a position to win is more important than most venture capitalists would like to admit.

For those that find themselves with investment positions at large, established venture capital firms with storied histories, stellar track records, and seemingly unlimited resources, it can be easy to rely on the firm's size, brand, or reputation as a key selling point for how you will add value to your investments. While being part of one of these firms may put you at an initial advantage, it is still important to think beyond what your firm provides and focus on your own personal competitive advantage as well. Smart entrepreneurs know that the reputation of a specific partner within a firm is just as important as the brand name. Large firms have strict performance standards for their individual partners, who are required to earn their keep to stay in their role. Signing on the dotted line with a partner who leaves their firm only a few years later can be the kiss of death for many companies, because they end up losing access to political and actual capital from that firm. In a worst-case scenario, having big-name existing investors who don't continue to back you as the company matures can serve as a negative signal to the market as well, causing other investors to think, "Well, if that famous VC doesn't think it's a good opportunity, why should I?"

It can be tempting to look for a template to follow when it comes to adding value—there is nothing more comforting than a formula or a recipe for success. However, each individual's journey is different, and breaking into venture capital requires building a game plan that leverages your unique strengths. In the next three chapters, we'll discuss how you can build a play-book that works for you.

Principle 7   Double Down on What Makes You Different

Principle 8   Prioritize Your Winners

Principle 9   Stay the Course

DOUBLE DOWN ON WHAT MAKES YOU DIFFERENT

Early in my journey of becoming a VC, I was convinced that being myself was not a viable option. I was young. I was female. I wasn't independently wealthy. I lacked experience in the industry. I was starting a fund, not working at a famous one. I didn't go to Stanford or get an MBA. I was living in Asia, and I didn't speak "Silicon Valley." I searched the entire globe (literally!) for someone else who had "made it" as a VC with a similar background whom I could emulate, but I came up empty-handed.

Especially in the 2010s, the adage "You can't be what you can't see" rang true for any inspiring investors who didn't fit into the typical "old boys' club" of venture capital. According to a 2015 dataset compiled by the Social Capital Partnership and *The Information*, nearly two-thirds of the top 71 investment funds had no women as senior investment team members. The same study revealed that only one venture capital firm with more than $1 billion in assets under management, Google Ventures, had a black senior investing partner at that time. Not only that, but the age of investing partners across all funds was solidly in the mid-40s. Sequoia Capital, often seen as the gold standard when it comes to venture capital, had no women on its 14-person senior investing team and an average age of 46.[1]

I was already discouraged by this lack of role models, and it certainly didn't help that the pathway I had chosen into venture—starting and raising my own fund from investors—involved an overwhelming amount of rejection. When I hired a man to translate some of my meetings with local investors in Asia, one prospective investor ignored me and instead greeted my employee, asking, "Oh, is this white lady your secretary?" I sat through countless meetings where the people across the table would make eye contact only with my male partners. I even signed into a Zoom with prospective investors on a different time zone, so I was at home at the time, and they actually burst out laughing and asked me to confirm my identity.

It wasn't just my gender that made me different. Having started my career on Wall Street and not in Silicon Valley, I also felt like an outsider with the tech community, which seemed to have its own private language and culture in which I was far from fluent. When I traveled to the Bay Area, my typical outfit of black jeans and a blazer stuck out in a sea of notoriously underdressed entrepreneurs and VCs. The Bay Area uniform seemed to be slouchy jeans, company T-shirts, sneakers made out of recyclable material, and ironically large glasses. Unlike in Asia, most people I would meet with would not introduce themselves, which I interpreted as some sort of strange power move, with the presumption that you already knew who they were and why they were important. Instead, they would typically spend the first few minutes of a meeting aggressively asking questions and then proceed to lean back in their chair and let you perform for them. They would drop names of people I didn't recognize and then watch carefully for my reaction. They would use terms like "crushing it" and "on fire." Even though everyone was speaking English, I still felt I was in completely new territory.

Part of the reason I wore slightly more formal clothes was because I was constantly being told I was too young to be successful in venture capital, and dressing casually would lead to comments like, "You look like you're still in high school!" I tried wearing glasses to look older, and I removed my graduation dates from my LinkedIn profile so nobody knew my exact age, but I felt like no matter what I did, I couldn't win. Years later, even after I successfully raised capital, built an entire portfolio of companies, and was named to the Forbes Asia 30 Under 30 in Venture Capital and Finance, I was told by a general partner at my firm at the time that my "problem" was that I "peaked too early." Apparently, even being successful could be converted into a point of criticism.

While speaking at a conference in New Zealand, I learned there was a term for this phenomenon of constantly being criticized for standing out—**tall poppy syndrome**. Just like a tall poppy gets chopped down for growing above the rest, anyone with notable achievements or impressive differentiation is cut down to size by their peers.[2] Not surprisingly, there are similar idioms in almost every other culture. In Japan, it is often said, "The nail that sticks up gets hammered down." A 2018 study found that 90 percent of those surveyed (mostly women) felt their achievements were undermined in the workplace. Nearly 50 percent noted that even their friends participated in silencing them after a success.[3] Putting a name to an experience was cathartic, but it still didn't dissolve the persistent feeling that I was fighting for a place in an industry that didn't want me to be part of it.

Although it's easy to look back on all my own moments of being cut down and fantasize about the perfectly witty "Fuck you!" response I could have given, or how I should have walked out of the room, or punched them in the face, none of those things occurred to me at the time. Instead, I thought, "What am I doing wrong? How can I approach this differently? What if I wore different shoes? Spoke differently? Gave off more of a confident bro vibe?" I changed my clothes. I tried to do phone calls instead of video calls, I brought my older, male partners to meetings, I emphasized my accomplishments wherever I could, but it felt like it was fruitless. At the end of the day, it was exhausting trying so hard not to be me.

Thanks to the small, but growing community of women in venture capital at the time, I spent a lot of time commiserating with other female VCs who were going through similar experiences. We would discuss at length, "How can we be more aggressive, how can we become better networkers, negotiators, and advocates? How can we do a better job of supporting each other? What strategies can we be employing to get the industry to see us differently?" Per the ethos of Sheryl Sandberg's *Lean In*, we were looking for tips and tricks to understand how we might, in fact, be responsible for unknowingly sabotaging our own success.

Then, one crisp fall day on a business trip in New York City, I sat down to coffee with another new fund manager with whom I had been connected through a mutual friend. "He's also doing the hard work of raising a fund, perhaps you two can trade notes and swap contacts," my friend shared as context when he made the introduction. John, an ex–finance executive turned entrepreneur who was now raising his first fund, already had all the trademarks of a typical VC insider—he had the uniform of faded jeans, Allbird sneakers, and slightly overgrown beard paired with a confident swagger. Despite sauntering into the coffee shop like he owned the place, John told me how difficult fundraising had been for him as a new fund manager. "That's refreshing to hear," I replied, somewhat surprised by his candor. Relieved to be in the company of someone else taking the harder path into the industry, I blurted out, "It's fucking hard raising a new fund, right?!" To this day, I still remember the look of empathy and authentic confusion on John's bearded face as he replied, "I know! And it really shouldn't be!"

I was struck by his response, which had no hint of the self-doubt I had internalized so deeply. Instead, his fundamental assumption was that if people didn't want to invest in his fund, it was *their* fault, not his. Perhaps it was because he believed more deeply that he belonged in venture capital and that he was entitled to at least get a chance to succeed. Perhaps it was because he saw other people who looked like him who had made it, and therefore knew it was possible he could do it himself. Either way, it was this moment when I realized that perhaps I should reconsider my position on why it seemed to be so hard to break into this highly selective industry. Perhaps, like John, I could absolutely be a great investor given the opportunity, and it was the venture capital ecosystem itself that was broken.

Although actively managing blind spots can be a strength when it comes to making good investment decisions, self-awareness is not a cure for systemic shortcomings that run far deeper than any one person's strategy for figuring out how to fit in. In believing that the stifling exclusivity of venture capital was somehow my fault, I was also embracing the belief that I could be in control of fixing it. Although the illusion of control can be empowering, it was ultimately unproductive because it resulted in a failure to recognize that there were structural challenges to breaking into venture capital as an outsider. As it turns out, I couldn't change the lack of diversity in venture capital by wearing a different outfit.

For the first time, I wondered, "What if I just accepted that the fact that I am a young, self-made woman with a liberal arts degree and a few years' experience building startups internationally? What if that makes me unusual, but not unsuitable, for venture capital? What if that was actually a good thing? What if I used my energy not to hide my differences, but to embrace my unique point of view? What if I stopped "leaning in" to a system that wasn't built for me to succeed? What if I instead leaned *out* and started building a new system that had diversity at its core, not as an add-on feature bolted on?" I decided that this was the moment I would stop minimizing my individuality. Instead, I would double down on what made me different and build my own playbook for tapping into the power of the venture capital ecosystem.

Once I stopped searching for someone to be my champion and became my own, I found I suddenly possessed the emotional and intellectual bandwidth to focus on how to use my youth, my eagerness, my empathy, my curiosity, and my lack of preconceived notions to my advantage. My energy was freed up to be creative about how I could access great deals, analyze them efficiently, and add value beyond what most investors were promising. My curiosity and determination created ripple effects within my network that brought me a variety of unique opportunities to invest, to be invested in, and to add value. I was more proactive, not reactive. I remembered why I wanted to be in this industry in the first place—to change it, not to blend in!

As part of this proactive strategy, I started doing more writing about what it's like to be a young female in technology and venture capital, and my articles were picked up by mainstream media publications like *Forbes, Inc.*, and *Recode.* I took a risk by talking about the reality of the challenges for girls and young women in the STEM field, and the response was resounding—I wasn't the only one! I received dozens of notes from women whom I knew and just as many that I didn't, telling me things like, "I'm so relieved that this happened to you, too" and "Your article inspired me to start a company" or "Thanks to what you wrote, I decided to start my own venture capital fund."

I remembered why I wanted to be in this industry in the first place—to change it, not to blend in!

Instead of hiding myself from people because I assumed they'd have a criticism of any kind, I invested time in building my own network of people with whom I connected and enjoyed working, who were like-minded and saw the voids in the industry not as flaws but as opportunities. I started running events for female founders and investors, ranging from bringing in exciting speakers to small group dinners centered around themes like scaling enterprise business models, and I committed to formally mentoring younger women in the industry through organizations like All Raise and Parity Partners, two burgeoning communities for women aspiring to break into venture capital. I invested my time in personal relationships with people who made me feel good about myself and my chosen path, and I built a team of incredible partners who constantly reminded me that being different was *a good thing*. They supported my writing, opened up doors within their own personal networks, and encouraged me to flip the script and embrace all aspects of my point of view.

"I wish someone told me that when a founder picks you, or a firm picks you as a member of their investment team, they're hiring you for your point of view," Jomayra Herrera told me as we discussed what it's like to be different within the venture capital ecosystem. She recalled, "When I first got into venture capital, I thought my main role was to support the partners at my firm, and I was slow to share my point of view and my perspective on where the world is going. Now, I know that being different helps me stand out from the crowd. I wish I had done that earlier on." This sentiment was woven throughout all of the interviews I conducted for the book.

Your success as an investor is directly tied to the ways in which you can expand the possibilities for your investments.

Having a different viewpoint can be an asset in any industry. However, it is especially beneficial in venture capital, where investing is not just about putting money behind companies, but also leveraging your skill set, network, and platform to influence outcomes. Unlike buying shares in public companies, where your investment results in a very small percentage ownership and no control or influence over a company's trajectory, venture capital investors earn real ownership and have very real power over what direction a business takes. Just as I learned with Company Y, demonstrating a differentiated ability to add value beyond capital is the only way to earn the opportunity to invest in the companies you believe will be winners. Your success as an investor is directly tied to the ways in which you can expand the possibilities for your investments—the trick is identifying how you can do that in ways that are distinct from everyone else. That requires recognizing, nurturing, and growing what makes you distinctive. I learned there is a tremendous amount of power in your differences, but you can only tap into it if you stop fighting your differences and start highlighting them.

Although diversity in venture capital may be novel, doubling down on what makes you different is a solid strategy for breaking in and succeeding in the industry. Don't know where to start? Here are some key questions you can ask yourself in order to stop fitting in and start standing out:

1. *What* do you know that other people don't?

2. *Who* do you know that other people don't?

3. What can you *do* that other people can't?

QUESTION 1

WHAT DO YOU KNOW THAT OTHER PEOPLE DON'T?

When we started raising our first funds at Fresco Capital and we were tasked with creating our first website and our first investor decks, we decided to do a working session to shape our brand, narrative, and materials. We booked a conference room in our favorite coworking space, and we hunkered down in this room with gray walls, no windows, a whiteboard, and a lot of Post-it Notes. We tried our best to remove our filters and write down any and all words and phrases that were unique to us as individuals and as a firm.

As someone with very little experience in venture capital itself, I gravitated toward my experience transitioning from a corporate professional at Goldman Sachs to an early member of a fast-growing startup in New York City. I wrote about how I had helped build an education technology business from the ground up, and specifically how I had turned a one-way ticket from New York to Hong Kong into a business with thousands of students, multiple languages, and real revenue. I knew what it was like to show up in a new place and not know anyone. I knew how to network in a new culture, get people to buy into your vision, recruit a team, and forge critical partnerships to fill in the gaps in your resource pool. I also knew how hard and isolating it was to do that without an established network of friends and family. I knew what it was like to wake up to a full day of emails from different time zones, and how to transform a sense of panic into a sense of determination.

This unique knowledge about how to navigate international expansion started to shape my narrative for what made me different and how we could add value as a firm. We could help with international expansion, from the personal challenges to the professional opportunities of identifying a new market, finding partnerships, and recruiting country managers. This ultimately became our ethos at Fresco Capital—we could help companies expand to new markets with efficiency, balance, and drive. Whether it came to winning room in a seed round or ensuring our pro rata rights in a follow-on round, our ability to be the boots on the ground in an unknown place was a critical ingredient in our formula for success.

Caribou Honig, cofounder of QED Investors and now my partner at SemperVirens Venture Capital, found himself with a similar lack of experience in venture capital when he and two partners founded QED after scaling a successful financial upstart, Capital One, in 2008. "We had not a day of proper venture capital experience among us," he recalled. "We were open with entrepreneurs and coinvestors that we were 'masquerading as investors.' We did, however, have decades of collective experience in performance marketing, banking, credit, and managing hypergrowth at scale, which meant we brought something different to the table." Not only did this unique knowledge set and experience help Caribou and his partners make big bets on companies like Credit Karma and Remitly, which are now worth billions of dollars, but it also helped them add value in a unique way. "We could assist them after we made the investment in a way that was complementary to the support from other VCs on the cap table," Caribou pointed out. Instead of getting caught up in

impostor syndrome—the belief that he did not deserve his position despite his accomplishments, or that his skill set was inadequate in some way—Caribou and his partners embraced what made them different by leaning on what they knew that other people didn't. That is, how to scale a fintech startup.

In order to highlight your knowledge base and differentiate it, think about the following things:

- What is the hardest thing you have ever done, or what is the accomplishment that you are most proud of? What did you learn in the process that others, particularly entrepreneurs, could benefit from?

- When you meet entrepreneurs and share your personal narrative, what part of your background or experience set are they most interested in? What are the key lessons or insights that you find yourself sharing over and over again?

- When your network makes an introduction, what are they highlighting to entrepreneurs? Sometimes other can help us hold up a mirror to ourselves—what do others see as the most compelling thing about you when connecting you to an entrepreneur?

- Has anyone ever asked you if they could "pick your brain," or have you ever done paid consulting or advising? If so, what are people looking to learn from you?

What are the patterns that emerge as you answer these questions? How can you take what others have found valuable about your unique knowledge set and add it into your personal narrative, as we discussed in Principle 2? Going even further, how can you leverage this unique knowledge set into an "offering" that would be value added for an entrepreneur you are investing in? If you can answer these questions for yourself and for others, you'll be well on your way to winning the investments that you are most excited about as well as setting them up for long-term success.

QUESTION 2

WHO DO YOU KNOW THAT OTHER PEOPLE DON'T?

As a foreigner living in Asia, it was easy to identify the ways in which my skill set was differentiated. To founders in the United States, I knew how to help them set up shop in Asia. To partners in Asia, I provided a key access point to the US startup ecosystem, an innovation powerhouse many investors and professionals were keen to learn from. Whether it was my knowledge set or my network, being in a physically different place made it very easy to stand out (for better and for worse).

In 2018, however, I moved back to the United States to establish myself in San Francisco. When I tried to continue using my personal narrative that emphasized my experience building companies internationally, I was disappointed to find that this "value add" was perceived as far less valuable in a rich startup ecosystem like Silicon Valley, especially given that I was no longer physically based in Asia. Although I was already several years into my venture capital career, I had to figure out how to reinvent myself to stay relevant and competitive in a new environment. I found myself back at the drawing board—both literally and figuratively. Armed with my Post-it Notes, I started the process of redefining what made me different and how I could add value. Luckily, this time the room had windows.

As I wrote down thoughts without a filter and stuck them up on the wall, I started to see a pattern. This time, my differentiation was less about *what* I knew, and more about *who* I knew. As the tech and venture capital ecosystem was still reeling from the revelations of the #metoo movement, there was a tremendous amount of public pressure on technology companies of all sizes to recruit more female employees. The same pressure was being applied for investment firms to recruit more female investors, and boards to recruit more female executives. Over the years, I had been actively investing in a network of peers, many of whom were female founders, operators, and investors. In my efforts to surround myself with like-minded women who shared a similar mission of changing the face of venture capital and the companies we were backing, I had been ahead of the curve. This proved to be a powerful new tool in my tool kit for providing value to companies and funds—I could instantly tap into a group of highly qualified women in a way most male investors couldn't.

As time went on and I started to evangelize my thesis and passion for the future of work through writing, speaking, and investing, I developed a valuable network of thought leaders and founders building in that space as well. That was how I met my current partner and the cofounder of SemperVirens, Robby Peters. When Robby started SemperVirens in 2018, he had very little experience investing in startups. However, he had spent the previous 10 years of his career building networks of human resources executives and leaders, first as a recruiter and then as a business development executive at a consulting firm. HR practitioners are the ultimate buyers of a lot of new technology for the future of work, and he quickly saw that his network was a highly differentiated competitive advantage when convincing founders to take capital from him over other investors. Through his personal network alone, he could make dozens of connections to potential customers, thereby accelerating sales momentum in a way that no other venture capital firm could offer. Today, at SemperVirens, we have formalized that network of end buyers into a platform of HR advisors whom our portfolio companies can tap into for advice, connections, and insight into how to speed up their go-to-market in a notoriously difficult customer base.

In a world where it's not always *what* you know, but *who* you know, think deeply about how your network is differentiated from other investors, and how you can leverage that network into a scalable winning strategy for your portfolio companies.

When it comes to figuring out how you can turn your network into a concrete value-add, consider the following questions:

- When you make a new connection and you are thinking about how you can add value to them, what type of people are you offering to introduce them to? Who within your network are entrepreneurs naturally most interested in meeting?

- What types of communities have you found yourself gravitating toward as you seek to surround yourself with like-minded peers in the industry? Asked another way, what types of networking events do you actually get excited about attending? What is differentiated about the people that attend and that you ultimately build relationships with?

- List out your top 10 high-quality connectors across the categories discussed in Principles 1 and 2—directors of accelerator programs, other investors, founders, and service providers. Who has referred you the highest quality deal flow, and to whom have you referred the highest quality deal flow? What are the key distinguishing features of these individuals? Is there anything that all or some of them have in common?

- Ask all (or at least a solid sample set) of the founders you have already invested in, "What is the most valuable connection I have made for you?" Was it another investor? An employee or key executive hire? An advisor? What was the result of the connection, and why was it valuable for them?

Although you can answer most of these questions yourself, getting outside of your own head and polling your network can be a powerful tool for validating your assumptions about where you are adding value through your network. You never know where you have created important connections—it may not have been through direct introductions but instead through communities or events you have played a role in building. Danielle Strachman, cofounder and general partner of 1517 Fund, recalled discovering the power of her network when she was still working in the nonprofit sector. "When we were at the Thiel Foundation, I started to realize just how valuable our network could be for entrepreneurs. One of the Thiel Fellows met a mentor at the foosball table at one of our events. That mentor ended up buying his company." If that's not value-add, I don't know what is, but Danielle wouldn't have known how differentiated her network was if she didn't follow up with the founders she was supporting. Don't be afraid to ask others to reflect on your differentiation—you may be surprised by their answers!

QUESTION 3

WHAT CAN YOU DO THAT OTHER PEOPLE CAN'T?

Both inside and outside of the industry, it is fair to say that venture capitalists don't have a great reputation. Our branding in the media and among entrepreneurs is often that we are moneygrubbing, easily distracted by shiny things, and willing to say anything to get a deal done. We speak in platitudes, don't follow through on our promises, and like to congratulate ourselves on things we didn't actually do. While I can't deny that this stereotype is grounded in some truth, I can assert that it makes it very easy to stand out by taking action. In addition to knowledge and network, a key differentiating factor to adding value is the ability to *get things done* that others can't or won't.

When fundraising or investing, my relative youth has always been a stumbling block. In an industry where the average general partner is in their mid-forties, it was sometimes challenging to impress entrepreneurs who assumed I had less accumulated knowledge than my older peers did.[4] Similarly, it was an uphill battle to convince limited partners that I could influence the outcomes of my investments despite not having any gray hair. I found this to be incredibly frustrating considering that, unlike many other older VCs, I did not have any family, pets, or plants that required my attention. I worked from the moment I woke up to the moment my head hit the pillow at night. When I was asked what neighborhood I lived in, I would reply that I actually lived on an airplane, because if I was needed, I'd drop everything and go. Because of my stage of life, I could do anything to get the job done.

Soon, I learned to harness this energy into a powerful narrative for convincing stakeholders that I was the right investor to work with. Yes, I was young, but that meant our incentives were aligned in ways that they weren't for older investors. I told founders up front that I was building my wealth, reputation, and portfolio alongside them. The outcome of their business might not matter much for a VC who has made hundreds of investments over the course of their career, but I was just getting started and each win mattered. My willingness to work harder than anyone else in the room became a strategic point of advantage I could leverage whenever needed.

As time has gone on, I have admittedly acquired some gray hairs, but my work ethic has not faded. That said, my life circumstances have evolved with my age and experience level. I am no longer a single, borderline burned-out twentysomething spending most of her time on airplanes. I now have a portfolio of nearly 100 investments that I am balancing, and I have a family waiting for me at home. Just like I found myself back at the drawing board after I relocated to San Francisco, I've also had to perpetually reevaluate what I can do for founders now that I'm not necessarily building my firm brick by brick alongside them. The time had come to go back to the drawing board, yet again.

In a fit of anxiety one day, I consulted my husband on what made me different since my youthful edge and burgeoning portfolio had bloomed into a more mature stage of life and larger cohort of investments. As I sometimes do, I expressed my vulnerability in the form of self-doubt, "What am I going to say when I'm speaking to founders? I feel like I'm less different than I used to be."

"Well," he said as he crossed his arms and looked at me across the kitchen island with his trademark intensity, "Maybe, sometimes, it's not what you say, it's just how you are." I was struck by how profound this simple statement was. As a Midwesterner who grew up always feeling like I was on the outside, I have an approachable and curious demeanor that many mistake for naivete. However, I aim to treat every founder and investor with respect, and often spend extraordinarily long periods of time getting on the phone or constructing an email to founders explaining why we are choosing not to invest in their company. I outline the key questions that we would need to have answered in order to gain conviction; or if we simply could never invest based on their sector or solution, I also tell them that (nicely). Many founders never respond, presumably pissed off by the rejection. Others come back with quippy replies like, "I can't wait to prove you wrong." Some express appreciation for the feedback and ask to keep in touch. Many of these companies I end up investing in years later. Either way, most venture capital investors simply ignore founders or never follow up and expect them to understand that their nonresponse is code for "I'm not interested." Instead, I take the time to share candid feedback because I believe it is the right thing to do, especially for entrepreneurs that might not be fluent in venture capital yet.

In other words, sometimes, it's not just what you do, but also how you do it. Often, people find things that are memorable about us that we may not realize. Some people have unbridled enthusiasm that is contagious. Other times, it's a tendency for a unique type of analysis that leaves an indelible impression. When I asked Sarah Smith, partner at Bain Capital Ventures, how she differentiated herself when meeting with new companies, she pointed out, "I realized very quickly that you can stand out easily by doing your research. Be open and vulnerable, personal, and approachable. It is easy to make an impression by just being human and being yourself."

Indeed, Sarah's warmth, authenticity, and thorough preparation have resulted in a reputation that precedes her as a coinvestor and a board member. She adds significant value to her investments by drawing upon decades of experience as a technology executive and investor, but she also does it in a way that sets the standard for building a company culture that has integrity at its core.

When it comes to identifying what you can *do* (and *how* you do it) that others can't, here are a few places to jump-start your process:

- When it comes to your experience working with startups, in whatever capacity that may be, what are the key results you've been responsible for? What was unique about those results—was it their magnitude? Their speed? Their accuracy?

* Are there any habits—daily, weekly, or monthly—that you see as integral to your professional persona? English poet John Dryden once said, "We make our habits, and then our habits make us." How do these regular activities shape you and your ability to add value to others?

* Poll your network or take stock of the emails where you've been introduced by others. What are the top three adjectives they'd use to describe you and the way you are? As Maya Angelou stated so eloquently, "People will forget what you said, people will forget what you did, but people will never forget how you made them feel."

You don't have to be a superhero or a rocket scientist to be a successful venture capitalist. You don't have to be part of the old boys' club, either. However, you do need to be differentiated. Identifying and leveraging your differences are precisely how you will win the opportunities you seek. If you put in the work to figure out what you know that others don't, who you know that others don't, what you can do that others can't, and how you operate in a unique way, you will find yourself equipped with a powerful tool kit for accessing, analyzing, and adding value to the companies you have ownership in. Going through this exercise of self-assessment and constant self-inventory is not only helpful for winning deals and influencing outcomes, but also as a lifelong process for adapting your differentiators as you change and grow. Most important, though, it will ultimately help you build your confidence as you navigate an ever-changing competitive landscape while being yourself.

BREAKTHROUGH TIPS FOR DOUBLING DOWN ON WHAT MAKES YOU DIFFERENT

- If you find people telling you that something is wrong with you or trying to cut you down to size, flip the script. How are their criticisms actually strengths? Whatever negative narratives are out there, show others how they're false.

- Build a community of peers who remind you to be resilient when the road gets rough and encourage you to double down on what makes you different, not hide it.

- Do the work to figure out what truly differentiates you by following the exercises outlined throughout the chapter. Poll your network and seek insight from those you trust who see you in ways that you may not be able to see yourself.

- Incorporate your unique qualities into your personal narrative so that you put them front and center when it comes to building deal flow, conducting due diligence, and showcasing how you can amplify the success of the companies you back.

- Figure out ways that you can go beyond *telling* people how you are different to *showing* them through your reputation, your portfolio, and your platform. Invest in building a system for converting your differentiation into a repeatable, scalable competitive edge for your investments.

PRIORITIZE YOUR WINNERS

When I lie in bed at night and attempt to clear my head for sleep, it is inevitable that thoughts of whatever is going wrong in my life or work start to slowly seep into the corners of my mind. It often starts as an innocent question, "What if I spent a little more time with that company, could I help them figure out what's going wrong?" Or perhaps it takes the form of an idea, "What if we ran an event for them, would that help them generate more revenue?" Before I know it, it's been hours since my head hit the pillow and I am still ruminating over why something isn't going the way I hoped it would. Eventually, my brain quiets down, allowing sleep to roll in as the night gives way to the next day. When my alarm goes off, I wake up with an intense drive to take action on my previous night's fixations as I have irrevocably convinced myself that I can get things back on track with a little more time, effort, and creativity.

After tiring myself out—literally and figuratively—by dwelling on the negative, I start to check in with other investors, wondering if they also found themselves filling their brain space and their calendar attempting to solve the problems within their portfolio. As it turns out, this tendency to dwell on the negative is a mindset that isn't limited to venture capital. In psychology, **negativity bias** is our brain's tendency to remember bad experiences more acutely than good experiences. As cited by Professor Clifford Nass, a communications professor at Stanford University, in a *New York Times* article on the topic, "The brain handles positive and negative information in different hemispheres. Negative emotions generally involve more thinking, and the information is processed more thoroughly than positive ones. Thus, we tend to ruminate more about unpleasant events—and use stronger words to describe them—than happy ones."[1]

Our brains' gravitational pull toward a "glass half empty" mentality extends directly into investing. **Loss aversion** is a well-documented form of irrational decision-making, as extensive studies have shown that individuals experience more pain from losing money than the joy they experience from gaining the same amount. In other words, you hate losing $5,000 more than you love making $5,000. Not only does your brain pull you in that direction, but the companies in your portfolio that are struggling will also naturally demand more of your attention. In an industry where we often tell companies we have invested in that we want to be their first call when something goes wrong, it is no surprise that when a business is not working, you will find yourself spending countless hours on the phone talking about why that is and what you can do about it.

In venture capital, falling victim to this bias can be disastrous for your returns because the upside potential of every investment you make is unlimited. Although the losses may hurt more, one extraordinary winner more than makes up the difference. Unless you make a conscious effort to prioritize what's already working—both in terms of *how* you add value to your portfolio as well as *which companies* you're adding value to—you will find that your thoughts, your time, *and* your capital are consumed by the problematic portions of your portfolio. In this chapter, we'll outline some concrete steps you can take to prioritize the teams, companies, and concepts that will ultimately lead to your long-term success.

- **STEP 1.** Embrace the power law and what it means for your portfolio.

- **STEP 2.** Identify your winners early.

- **STEP 3.** Focus on winning strategies for adding value.

- **STEP 4.** Know when—and how—to (gracefully) walk away.

STEP 1

EMBRACE THE POWER LAW AND WHAT IT MEANS FOR YOUR PORTFOLIO

You may have noticed already how much venture capitalists *love* to use the term "the power law." This is partially because, in this industry, it's considered very cool to casually drop terms that other people probably don't understand. Using esoteric language communicates a sense of superiority and gauges the other person's fluency in tech lingo, which is often mistaken as a legitimate proxy for how connected, experienced, and intelligent they are. The other reason is that the power law is indeed one of the most important concepts to grasp if you want to have anything to do with venture capital.

You may remember that we first talked about the power law in Principle 4 in the context of analyzing the total addressable market (TAM) of a potential investment, but we will revisit it here because it has important implications for how to prioritize your portfolio. The **power law** can be boiled down to a relationship where one variable yields a disproportionately large impact on the result. In other words, the relationship is not linear, it is exponential. If a company is able to increase its revenue consistently, say 1.3x year over year, then its growth would follow a linear pathway (see Figure 8.1). However, if a company is able to double its revenue every year, its growth trajectory follows a **power curve** because the growth can be modeled by the regression $y = x^2$ (x to the second power). Growth on a power curve is exponential, and the company will become very big very quickly.

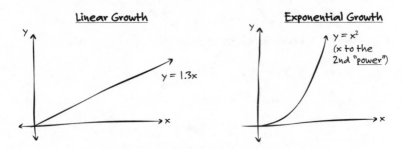

Figure 8.1 Linear versus exponential growth

In the context of venture capital, this means that even just one investment that is following a power curve can and will have a disproportionately large impact on the returns of the entire portfolio. If one of your investments does *extremely* well, so will your entire portfolio. By extension, any companies that are *not* generating exponential results are relatively meaningless to your ultimate performance. I have experienced this firsthand with several of my funds. Because I usually invest at the early stage, when companies are worth $50 million or less, my portfolio metrics look very good once at least one company is valued at $1 billion or more. We will discuss portfolio performance metrics in more depth in Principle 9: "Stay the Course," but one of the key ways of measuring returns on a fund is the multiple on invested capital (MOIC). When we invested in the seed round of a company that went on to be valued at $1.3 billion, our fund MOIC went from 1.2x to 5x, which is considered to be very good. It only took one company with exponential growth to transform our return profile from mediocre to exceptional.

If you recall the example of Y Combinator highlighted in Principle 4, they calculated that only two of their investments resulted in 75 percent of their returns over the course of seven years.[2] This concept is especially important to understand when it comes to figuring out how to leverage your personal and professional strengths into a financially successful portfolio, because it means that a winning portfolio strategy starts with identifying which companies are most likely to generate exponential outcomes and therefore drive the majority of your returns and focusing most of your time, energy, and resources on maximizing those outcomes. We'll come to that next.

This should make sense in theory, but you still might not believe me, so let's look at the numbers, which really drive the point home (Tables 8.1 and 8.2). Assume that you have 19 companies in the portfolio. Let's say that you work your ass off and you prevent any single company from going to zero—good for you! You ultimately are able to achieve 1x to 2x on most of these companies, and you even get two 5x winners in the portfolio. That's Scenario 1. In Scenario 2, almost every single company in your portfolio goes to zero. One of them, however, exits for 100x your initial investment. Let's take a look at how much money you make in each scenario. For simplicity's sake, I am ignoring dilution and assuming that you write the same check size into each company and earn 20 percent carry on returns only after you have returned all initial capital to your investors.

Table 8.1 Scenario 1: A Portfolio Where *No* Company Goes to Zero

Company	Investment Size	Exit Multiple	Exit Value
1	$100,000	1	$100,000
2	$100,000	1	$100,000
3	$100,000	1	$100,000
4	$100,000	1	$100,000
5	$100,000	1	$100,000
6	$100,000	1	$100,000
7	$100,000	1	$100,000
8	$100,000	1	$100,000
9	$100,000	1	$100,000
10	$100,000	1	$100,000
11	$100,000	1	$100,000
12	$100,000	1	$100,000
13	$100,000	1	$100,000
14	$100,000	1	$100,000
15	$100,000	1.5	$150,000
16	$100,000	2	$200,000
17	$100,000	1	$100,000
18	$100,000	5	$500,000
19	$100,000	5	$500,000
Totals	$1,900,000	1.5	$2,850,000
Return to GP: $190,000*			

*Return is calculated as follows:

$2,850,000 in exit value minus $1,900,000 initial capital returned to investors equals $950,000 in profit. GP earns 20% carry on profits which equals $190,000.

Table 8.2 Scenario 2: A Portfolio Where Lots of Companies Go to Zero, Except for *One* that Does Very Very Well

Company	Investment Size	Exit Multiple	Exit Value
1	$100,000	0	$0
2	$100,000	0	$0
3	$100,000	0	$0
4	$100,000	0	$0
5	$100,000	0	$0
6	$100,000	0	$0
7	$100,000	0	$0
8	$100,000	0	$0
9	$100,000	0	$0
10	$100,000	0	$0
11	$100,000	0	$0
12	$100,000	0	$0
13	$100,000	0	$0
14	$100,000	0	$0
15	$100,000	0	$0
16	$100,000	0	$0
17	$100,000	0	$0
18	$100,000	0	$0
19	$100,000	100	$10,000,000
Totals	$1,900,000	5.3	$10,000,000
Return to GP: $1,620,000			

*Return is calculated as follows:

$10,000,000 in exit value minus returning $1,900,000 initial capital to investors equals $8,100,000 in profit. GP earns 20% carry on profits which equals $1,620,000.

The numbers highlight an irrefutable truth about venture capital: one winner more than makes up for all the losers at once. Even though our brains are hardwired to dwell on the pain of negative experiences over positive ones, and we have an inherent instinct to avoid losses, a portfolio with *no* losses can be far worse than a portfolio where 18 out of 19 investments goes to zero! Essentially all of the 1x, 2x, and even 5x returns don't make a difference at all. It's the 100x that matters.

Figuring out the big winners and prioritizing them can be straightforward when you are building a portfolio from the ground up, but it can be slightly more complex if you are joining an existing firm that has already deployed capital into companies that you are then expected to add value to. This is known as **inheriting a portfolio**, meaning you are now a part owner of a set of companies in which you did not necessarily make the decision to invest. As a new or younger employee now part of a team managing a preexisting portfolio, it is very common to get assigned to "fix" or "monitor" investments in companies that are struggling. This can be an informal process, which involves spending time with those founders, meeting members of their executive team, or analyzing their financials in order to identify the right business levers to pull to improve performance. At firms that lead investment rounds and join boards for governance purposes, it can take on a more formal tone where a new associate or principal is assigned to attend or run board meetings as well. I speak from experience when I say that these opportunities can be invaluable learning experiences, but they also mean taking time away from investing time and energy in investment opportunities that are more likely to generate outsized returns and lead to long-term success in the industry.

For Kyle Lui, the first board he joined as a new investor at DCM Ventures was a company the firm had invested in eight years prior. The company had several years of flat or slightly negative growth, which is the death knell for companies with venture capital investors who are seeking hypergrowth. As Kyle described it to me, "It was clear the company was not going anywhere." Given that this was his first board seat, he couldn't exactly blow it off, but he did figure out very quickly that he needed to be wise about how he was investing his time and energy. "Part of me was hoping I could turn the ship around and reignite growth, but at some point it became clear that wasn't possible," he told me, "Although it was hard, I was really disciplined about managing my time so I could focus on the companies that had the potential to drive returns."

That desire to be the one who saves the day can be very compelling. Whether or not they are willing to admit it, everyone dreams of being the hero.

However, Kyle knew better than to play a superhero. Instead of dwelling on the negative or putting more money and time into a company that was clearly not working, he shifted his focus onto finding new investments and adding value to other companies in the portfolio that were already doing well—a strategy that ultimately paid off.

That desire to be the one who saves the day can be very compelling. Whether or not they are willing to admit it, everyone dreams of being the hero.

"In the end, the company I was on the board of got acquired for $0.20 on the dollar. I was really glad I didn't spend every minute of my time with them," Kyle said. He learned firsthand that this type of subpar returns (less than 1x) would make very little difference to his reputation and performance as a VC, and even less of a difference to the success of the fund itself. Of course, you must have compassion for all the hard work that goes into building a business over the years, but it's important to remember that money matters, and anything less than 100x is pretty much the same as 0x. Embracing that reality and allocating your time and capital accordingly is a critical part of breaking into venture capital with success.

STEP 2

IDENTIFY YOUR WINNERS EARLY

So, now you have embraced the power law mentality and created an awareness that you need to override the gravitational pull of spending all your time, energy, and capital on companies whose returns won't matter in the long run. Fantastic! But wait . . . how do you know which are the companies that are going to drive your returns, and which are the ones that won't? Of course, when you first invest in a business, you, the founders, and all your coinvestors need to believe that it will be one of your massive winners. When will you know if it is worth continuing to invest in? Some exits take 10 or more years to return capital to their investors, but you have tens of thousands of hours to allocate in the meantime! Although nothing is over until the money hits your bank account, you can typically start to differentiate between the winners and the losers in your portfolio sooner than you might think.

In addition to talking about the power law without explaining what it means, venture capitalists also love to say, "Winners keep on winning." As someone who has identified with being a perpetual outsider, I've always resented this phrase because it implies that it is impossible to break into venture capital unless you're already part of the club. After all, if the only way to get ahead is by already being ahead, how can you possibly get started?

However, I have also come to appreciate this saying's accuracy and relevance for figuring out where to add value within your portfolio. The concept that people, companies, or ideas that have already started to demonstrate success are highly likely to continue down that path is more eloquently explained by scientists as **preferential attachment**. While this has been observed anecdotally by sociologists as far back as biblical times, it has started to be formally documented as part of an emerging field of study known as **network science**, or the study of how connections between things impact outcomes at both the cellular and the sociological level.

Dr. Alexander Gates is one of the leading academics on the forefront of understanding how networks operate, so I sat down with him to better understand the science behind how preferential attachment works, why it means that winners keep on winning, and how that leads to power law distributions in venture capital. As an assistant professor of data science at the School of Data Science at the University of Virginia, Dr. Gates is an expert at boiling complex concepts down and explaining how they work in the real world. In my personal life, I know him simply as Alex, since he happens to be my brother-in-law. He explained that in science, this concept is called "Success breeds success," and it is a well-documented phenomenon evident in everything from academic research (research papers that are already cited by other authors tend to get mentioned more often in new research), tweets (once a tweet gets liked and retweeted a lot, it is more likely to go viral), and songs (once a song has been streamed a lot, it is highly likely to continue to generate listens). I could hear the excitement in Alex's voice as he talked about how the patterns he observes in a laboratory setting play out predictably in real life.

Most interestingly, Alex pointed to a famous example about how ideas get funded. A Dutch experimental sociologist by the name of Arnout van de Rijt conducted an experiment on Kickstarter, where he randomly selected 200 new Kickstarter projects with zero donations so far, none of which he knew personally nor had any connection to. He donated a small amount of money to half, which were randomly chosen, and nothing to the other half. Arnout found that the projects that received his initial donation were two times more likely to attract further funds than those that did not receive his initial donation.[3] "What is most interesting about this," Alex said, "is that even a completely random signal of success—like a random donation on Kickstarter—is amplified over time. In venture capital, it is important to recognize that there is also an element of randomness at play. Is it the best companies that do well right away, or is it just the lucky ones? It doesn't really matter because after the first few data points, it's the success itself that is most relevant, not necessarily how or why it happened." In other words, if you want to predict which companies will achieve exponential growth, all you need to do is spot the ones that are doing well early on.

When he told me about this concept, I racked my brain for an example of a company in my portfolio that had successfully "turned things around" after a few tough years. I couldn't recall any specifics, but I thought surely I must have heard anecdotes from other investors about companies that they had written off as sure losers that came back from behind to surprise them. A more in-depth analysis of my investments, however, confirmed that this concept of coming back from behind has *never* been the case. In fact, even as an early stage investor, it takes only a few quarters from the time I invest to be able to see the signals of where early success is most likely to breed future success.

So then, what exactly should you be looking for when it comes to early signals of success?

"Growth," Alex emphasized. "In science, we use the rate of growth as the primary indicator of future success. Is the growth rate itself increasing? If you have preferential attachment dynamics, growth will be accelerating."

At the time of investment, be sure to identify what key metrics will ultimately drive the company's success and look for early signals that those metrics are outperforming.

Venture capital is not always the same as science, but I agree with Dr. Gates that revenue growth is the most important driver to watch when it comes to identifying which companies you should be spending your time on. That said, each company is different. In some cases, it may be account creation, daily engagement numbers, or contracts signed. At the time of investment, be sure to identify what key metrics will ultimately drive the company's success and look for early signals that those metrics are outperforming. I tend to place significant emphasis not only on early success in absolute terms, but also relative to projections. Has a team hit or beat their projected goals? If so, they're likely to continue to do so, and you should be finding ways to add value however you can.

STEP 3

FOCUS ON WINNING STRATEGIES FOR ADDING VALUE

In the last chapter, we discussed the importance of doubling down on what makes you different as the best way to stand out from the crowd, compete for the best deals, and ultimately add value in a way that uniquely contributes to the success of your investment. Whether it's what you know, who you know, or just how you are, it's important to channel your individual strengths into a platform for tipping the scales in favor of your portfolio. As you embark on this journey of figuring out where you can add value, it takes some additional filtering to find the overlap between how you can add value that is *differentiated*, how you can add value is in a way that *makes a difference*, and how you can add value in a way that *brings you energy*. The combination of these three criteria equates to a winning strategy for accelerating the growth of your portfolio companies. Just like you need to prioritize winners within your portfolio, you also need to prioritize winning strategies for adding value.

That will ensure not only that you increase the magnitude of your wins, but also the impact you have on them—a key element when it comes to making the argument that your capital is more valuable than just the dollar amount, which is ultimately what allows you to access great deals in the future.

Many years ago, when I first started thinking about how I could add value to my portfolio companies, I saw a lot of other venture capitalists focusing heavily on adding value through financial analytics support. Many budding VCs were leveraging their investment banking skill sets by helping founding teams build financial models and better understand how various factors would impact their long-term growth. Although I do have this skill set, I was immediately bored and drained by the idea of spending more time than I needed to in Microsoft Excel. Because others were focused on adding value in this way, I didn't think I could make a difference by focusing on it as well. Plus, I hated it, which meant I probably wouldn't actually do it well, or continue to do it in the future.

In his book *Go Put Your Strengths to Work: 6 Powerful Steps to Achieve Outstanding Performance*, leading work researcher and cocreator of the StrengthsFinder Assessment, Marcus Buckingham, points out that what you are good at, or what makes you different, is not the same as your "strengths." Instead of defining strengths as "what you are good at," he suggests instead focusing on what gives you energy. Something is a strength if it makes you feel successful, you are drawn to it, it fully engages you when you are doing it, and you feel energized and powerful after you are finished.[4] If you can throw your full weight behind your natural strengths, you are more likely to continue to develop those skills (and as a result, get better over time), as well as continue to work harder for your portfolio companies because, well, you enjoy it!

Just like I knew Excel spreadsheets wouldn't be my thing, I needed to figure out what tangible skills I could bring to the table on behalf of my portfolio companies that also energized me and would keep me motivated to continue honing my craft of adding value. As Buckingham recommends in his book, I reached back into my professional history for clues about what my true strengths might be.

The first conference I ever attended when I was working on building General Assembly's education technology business in Asia was a Startup Weekend event in Hong Kong. There were several hundred people there, and I was tasked with collecting as many email addresses as possible to contribute to our marketing list, as email marketing was a reliable way for us to build an audience and reach students in a new market. I was excited by the possibility of accomplishing so much at one event, but the truth is that although I am generally a friendly person, being in large crowds gives me intense anxiety. I seek back rows at concerts, always prefer to be on an end seat, and obsessively alter my schedule to avoid rush hour. I don't even like big parties with large groups of friends. In these environments, my introverted nature takes over and I am quickly exhausted by the repetitive small talk and lack of authentic connections.

This time, though, I was motivated to make it out to the event because I had been given a speaking slot, where I was asked to talk about the importance of technology skills and entrepreneurial communities for pursuing a fulfilling career path. Unfortunately, I wasn't aware that I was the only English speaker at the conference and all other speakers were using the audience's native Cantonese. Given that Hong Kong is a former British colony, and all higher education is done in English, most working professionals in Hong Kong do speak English, but how could I be sure? I distinctly remember the moment on stage when I looked out into the audience and realized that I was unable to interpret their reactions to my speech. Were they enjoying it? Was this resonating? Were they totally bored? My memory collapsed under the weight of my own insecurity, and before I knew it, I was completely at a loss for what I was planning to say next. My fight-or-flight response kicked in, and I rushed through the rest of my slides—reading them word for word—until I was done, at which point I rushed off stage and promptly left the venue to go straight home.

As a once aspiring actress (though unfortunately my career was limited to playing an oddly high number of clowns, supporting roles in high school plays, and a commercial for a local golf dome in Addison, Illinois), I was devastated by my onstage humiliation. From the safety of solitude in my 200-square-foot apartment, I penned a blog post about how much I hated conferences, how embarrassed I was by my experience on stage, and lamenting the disconnect between what I wanted to say and what I actually said, and solicited tips on public speaking. Much to my surprise, the blog post found a larger audience than I expected and sparked some really meaningful conversations about the value of putting yourself out there, learning from it, and getting better as a result. I didn't get the email addresses I needed by schmoozing at the conference, but I did get them through my writing about it.

Recalling this experience crystallized for me Buckingham's point about finding your strengths by focusing on what gives you energy and minimizing exposure to what drains you. If I tried to focus all my time and energy on "networking" at conferences or speaking to audiences I didn't know, I wouldn't last very long, nor would I be likely to reach my goals. Instead, if I focused on things that I enjoyed and felt natural to me—like writing—the end results were always better. Although the process started in solitude, it usually ended in more meaningful connections than being surrounded by people.

Armed with this new information about my strengths, not just as a venture capitalist but also throughout my entire career, I have applied this strategy to accessing, analyzing, and adding value in my role as a VC. Writing has served as a key tool in my ability to vocalize my thesis and what I am looking for in investments, which has helped bring great opportunities my way. Furthermore, writing requires synthesizing and articulating my beliefs, which has forced me to solidify my selection criteria for investments. And finally, building a brand and cultivating a reputation as a thoughtful investor well versed in the future of work has helped me win competitive deals. It has helped me build an audience and create connections that I can leverage on behalf of my portfolio companies as well, a critical asset in my ability to add value post-investment. When you focus on what brings you energy, even if it's not what you might originally have anticipated, you will find you have an incredible ability to help your winners keep on winning.

STEP 4

KNOW WHEN—AND HOW—TO (GRACEFULLY) WALK AWAY

Prioritizing winners within your portfolio, as well as prioritizing winning strategies for adding value, inherently means that there will be both companies and skill sets that will be *de*prioritized. In an industry where your reputation and your brand are everything, how do you allocate your time efficiently without acting like the very same ass-holes that I have advised you to avoid? Whether you are choosing not to invest in a company where you have already invested a significant amount of time in due diligence, shifting resources and energy away from a company where you have already invested but they have not demonstrated signs of exponential growth, or changing tack when it comes to how you leverage your skill set to add value, it is critical to know when and how to gracefully walk away.

The first step to avoiding a difficult situation is sometimes trust-ing your intuition and walking away before things even have a chance to go sour. Although it's never a good look to regularly renege on commitments, if you have a gut feeling something is not going to go well, it's better to pass before it's too late. Not only does that prevent having to make tough decisions later, but walking away from a deal that feels like a bad fit can free up your time and energy to focus on better ones. Kyle Lui, partner at DCM Ventures, recalled a company he met early in his career. "The traction was there but the founder rubbed me the wrong way. When I passed on investing, he sent me an antagonistic email and it left a very sour taste in my mouth." Although that company is worth billions of dollars today, Kyle insists that he does not regret not investing because it would have been a very taxing relationship. "I need to be able to partner with a founder for the long term. We don't always have to see eye-to-eye, but we need to be able to work together," he emphasized.

Sarah Smith, partner at Bain Capital Ventures, defines this pro-cess as **identifying your nonnegotiables**. In other words, what are the reasons you'd walk away from a deal, even if it could potentially be very lucrative for you? When I asked her about hers, she said, "Trust in a founder is a nonnegotiable for me. If I am going to be recruiting the best people in my network to go work for this founder, I need to have total trust in them. Many other VCs don't feel that way, and they are fine working with founders in a different way. Figure out what your nonnegotiables are and stick to them." For some investors, nonnegotiables may be fact-based, such as how a company is structured, if a founder lives in the same city as you, or how they allocate equity to their employees. For others, like Sarah, they are values-based.

I fall in Sarah's category—most of my nonnegotiables are based on values. For example, respect. Two years ago, I walked away from an investment in a company I'll call Company D. The company was building a platform for efficiently hiring and paying international contractors, something that has historically been prohibitively expensive and logistically challenging (and after spending so many years in Asia, I would know!). The business was demonstrating early signs of momentum, and it was becoming clear that they were on the path for exponential growth. However, during the investment process, the founder did not treat me and my team with respect. He was difficult to communicate with, ignored key requests for information, and was rude in our meetings. Although the business checked all of our boxes, we ultimately decided not to invest, and it is now a proud part of my anti-portfolio. If a founder is difficult to work with when things are going well, they are very likely to be even worse when things are challenging.

Even if the company isn't going to make or break your portfolio, you can't simply ignore and abandon companies that aren't doing well.

Unfortunately, knowing when and how to walk away from a company that is not working is more challenging when you have already invested. Although drawing these boundaries is essential for long-term success, it is also true that regardless of its performance, every company you invest in is composed of a team that has poured their blood, sweat, tears, and years into building their business. Even if the company isn't going to make or break your portfolio, you can't simply ignore and abandon companies that aren't doing well.

As Joe Floyd at Emergence Capital put it, "You make your money on your winners, but you make your reputation on your losers. How you treat entrepreneurs and how you help them find that soft landing is very important."

As a reminder, a **soft landing** is an exit, most commonly a merger or acquisition, that is not meaningful financially for anyone involved but helps a company, its product, and its founders find a new home and save face by being able to claim that they were acquired. If an exit returns less than 1x to its investors, it is definitely a soft landing. By contrast, a **hard landing** would be declaring bankruptcy or shutting down the company altogether.

Whether it is a blockbuster IPO, a multibillion-dollar acquisition, or a soft landing, the board of directors plays a critical role in facilitating and negotiating the terms of an exit. *Especially* if the resulting proceeds are *not* meaningful for your fund, entrepreneurs take note of how they were treated in the process. Joe advised that his policy is that you should always be generous with founding teams when you can. In his playbook, being generous means ensuring that the exit terms allow for the founders get a **carveout**, which is some sort of payment even though their equity might be worth nothing.

A carveout takes some of the capital being paid for the company and proactively allocates it to founders, even if their investors have a 1x liquidation preference that would typically require all proceeds to go to investors up until they receive their full investment amount back. As Joe explained, "If a company is selling for $0.30 on the dollar, you might as well give the management team a good carveout because it's not going to make a difference to us. Smart institutional investors get that."

Even if you don't have the power to change the terms of an exit deal, being generous also means being human and remaining sensitive to the fact that while you might have a portfolio of companies, a founder has only one. Figuring out how to walk this fine line— the line between investing most of your time and energy into your big winners, while also being respectful of those that aren't likely to make the cut—requires integrity and authenticity. I would never recommend telling a founder, "I think you are going to fail, so I can't spend time with you anymore." However, sometimes there is a need for a straightforward conversation regarding the state of the business. Start by asking the CEO some probing questions to understand how they are synthesizing their lackluster growth. Do they believe that the challenges they are facing are fixable, or are they beyond the team's control? Do they want to continue to commit their own time, capital, and energy into building something that isn't working? Are they open to hearing the feedback that it may be time to explore ways to move on? I have found that more often than not, the leadership is aware they are not set up to win, but they are afraid to admit that to their investors. If you provide them with an opening, they may share that they are on the same page.

However, if that isn't the case, then creating concrete boundaries can be helpful for ensuring you don't get sidetracked by the gravitational pull of a troubled business. Set up regular, quarterly check-ins with a founder. Be focused and available during your predetermined time together, but reduce your time allocation in between those meetings. Continue to add value where you can, but only in ways that don't require huge time investments. For example, make introductions, but don't spend hours back-channeling influencers in the way you might for a big winner in your portfolio.

When I was raising my first fund, an LP who passed on investing told me, "Before I invest in your fund, I need to see that you have had a big success in your portfolio, and I need to see that your fingerprints are all over it."

I resented hearing the no at that time, but I have never forgotten that conversation. Although we have learned that it helps to demonstrate an early win, investing in one hugely successful company can be written off as dumb luck and is not enough to build a long-term career in venture capital. Instead, you need to add value to your top performing portfolio companies in ways that moves the needle for their business—and yours. That requires watching for early signals of success, drawing boundaries both before and after you've invested, and focusing on strategies that leverage your unique strengths. That is much more than getting lucky—it is the art and the science of venture capital.

BREAKTHROUGH TIPS
FOR PRIORITIZING YOUR WINNERS

- Take the time to regularly model out how the power law will impact the returns for your overall portfolio. Based on recent performance, what type of outcomes are you anticipating for each portfolio company, and how might that eventually flow back to you in the form of carry? This will serve as a strong reminder that anything less than 10x is not likely to make a difference to you and should not be where you are investing the majority of your time.

- Closely track growth rates on a quarter over quarter basis, as well as relative to projections. Are they increasing? If so, consider increasing your time and money invested in that company.

- Make a list of your strengths and weaknesses, not just defined by what you're good at, but also what gives you energy. Spend more time and resources adding value in ways that you enjoy and also demonstrate results.

- Identify your nonnegotiables *before* you make an investment. Whether they are fact-based or values-based, write them down, and don't be afraid to pass on investing if the company doesn't meet your criteria. It will save you a lot of time and energy in the future.

- Keep track of how your value-add is impacting the businesses in your portfolio. Is it working? Are you helping them achieve their business goals? If yes, continue. If not, consider changing your priorities.

STAY THE COURSE

When I started writing this book, I reached out to some of my favorite investors in the industry—my peers, friends, and collaborators—many of whom, like me, worked hard to break into venture capital despite not having the typical background that has historically dominated the industry. Some of them are featured in these pages, but many more of them declined to be interviewed for fear of "sending a message that they had *made it* in venture capital" when they believed they hadn't. I heard, "I wouldn't want to pretend that I am more successful than I am," or "There are probably others that are better qualified to speak on the topic," or "I'm still learning, so I'm probably not the best person." The list of reasons they did not consider themselves to be experts goes on and on. In an industry where confidence and its close relative, arrogance, are practically part of the job description, I was surprised to find such pervasive insecurity lurking right below the surface. Was it merely a case of classic impostor syndrome, or was there something deeper to this divergence between how we as VCs project our success versus how we internalize it?

The more I turned this problem over in my mind, however, the more deeply I could relate to being unsure about my own skill set as a venture capitalist, not because of my own insecurity but because the true and absolute measure of success—the returns on your investments—can take more than a decade to come to fruition. As a result, it took me years to believe that I was qualified to teach or write about venture capital at all. Writing this book was part of countless New Year's resolutions, birthday resolutions, and goal setting exercises. Whenever I sat down to craft an outline of the proposal, I thought about the headlines I'd read on a daily basis telling how my peer from another firm had been on CNBC that day, had been named to the Forbes Midas List, or had raised a $150 million debut fund as a solo investor (mine was more like $10 million, and I had two partners). I thought about the exits from my portfolio, the amount of money I had personally made, and the amount of capital I had returned to investors over the years and wondered if they were really big enough to warrant "successful" as an adjective, especially when I knew that others had accomplished so much more (or at least their PR teams said they did).

I'd get a few pages into writing, and memories of the rejections I had received over the years would come flooding back. The prospective investors in our funds that said, "Your returns look great on paper, but I only believe them after you've returned cash." Or once we returned cash to our investors, the ones who said, "That's great, but how do I know you can do it more than once?" Or when I interviewed at larger venture funds who said, "That's a great track record, but is it really yours? Or was it only possible because of your partners?" or "That's a great portfolio, but it's not relevant because you sourced it when you were living in Asia, and now you live here, so how do we know you can replicate it?" After years of everyone else questioning my ability to succeed in such a complex industry, how could I not suffer at least a few cracks in my confidence?

If you feel like you are constantly being judged, that's because you are. After all, venture capital is an industry where success is literally defined by how good your judgment is. Whether it's where you invest your time, who you decide to include in your network, or how you evaluate an investment opportunity, making good decisions is a core part of the job description. Naturally, by extension, making good decisions means asking a lot of questions, formulating an opinion with conviction, and ultimately always remaining open to revisiting your convictions when presented with data that suggests otherwise. If you're not careful, constant exposure to this never-ending feedback loop can result in a broken internal barometer for success.

> **Venture capital is an industry where success is literally defined by how good your judgment is.**

Of course, there is also plenty of competitive sabotage—many see this game as competitive and not collaborative and will do anything to cut you down, break your spirit, instill insecurity, gaslight, or generally insult you based on who you are as a person or where you come from. In either case, whether it's judgment that comes with the territory or inappropriate judgment from assholes that seem to permeate the industry no matter how hard we try to avoid them, the only antidote is to stay the course. There is one surefire way to lose in venture capital, and that is to quit.

In this chapter, we'll discuss strategies for how to shield yourself from doubts (even when they're in your own head), cultivate your own sense of confidence, and remain true to yourself so that you can continue to review, revise, and reinvent the way you perform at your job. If you can do that, you will not only break into venture capital, but you will stick around long enough to thrive within it. Heck, if I have a say in it, you might even leave it a little bit better than you found it.

1. Accept the power of perception.

2. Create benchmarks for your process.

3. Look for collaborators, not role models.

4. Just keep going.

STEP 1

ACCEPT THE POWER OF PERCEPTION

If you are paying attention to the world of venture capital, you can easily fall down a rabbit hole of success stories. When I was meeting with hundreds of investors to piece together $50,000 investments into our first fund, while also navigating a myriad of health challenges due to my constant travel across time zones, it was a huge bummer to constantly be bombarded with headlines in venture capital press like "So-and-So Raises $100 Million Debut Fund" or "How This Venture Capitalist Made Millions on a Single IPO" or scrolling through my Twitter feed with well-meaning but overly simplistic "How-to" threads on "Here's how to raise $80 million in two months." My head hurt from all of my exaggerated eye rolls, but mostly my heart hurt from constantly wondering how it could be possible that everyone else was constantly crushing it except for me!

Even worse, when I tried to open up to others about the challenges and uncertainty I was facing, it was met with the sympathetic "I hear you" and "Gosh, that must be tough" but nobody ever seemed to reciprocate with sharing their pitfalls. I still distinctly remember a coffee meeting with another VC right after I moved to San Francisco when I was trying to figure out my next step. I poured my heart out to her, expressing my doubt regarding the ability to move forward with our current fund strategy, and the uncertainty I felt regarding whether I really knew what I was doing or if I should spend time at a more traditional fund to learn how venture capital was supposed to be done. I looked up from my almond milk latte to find her looking at me with a grimace that was a hybrid between pity and disgust. She sighed uncomfortably and gently shook her head, and she said, "Yeah, I don't know . . . that really sucks, sorry, I don't really know what to tell you." I felt completely lost and humiliated, awkwardly wrapping up the meeting never to hear from her again. Was I just a persistent pessimist who was constantly focused on my failures instead of finding motivation from my small wins? Unfortunately, this crisis of attitude made me feel worse—how did everyone else seem so positive and upbeat all the time?

What I began to realize is that the *perception* of success in venture capital is just as important as *actual* success. Because venture capital transactions are all private, there is basically no way of ever knowing what anyone else's *actual* returns are. All you really know about the success of another VC or their firm is what they choose to tell you. It is impossible to differentiate between performance and perception.

This phenomenon where perception becomes reality is another foundational principle in **network science**, or the study of relationships between things, that I discussed with Dr. Alex Gates of the School of Data Science at the University of Virginia in Principle 8. Network scientists have done extensive research on the correlation between performance and success in fields ranging from art to academia. Their findings indicate that when performance can't be measured, networks drive success.[1] In other words, success is not just about the person being measured, it is also determined by their network and how that network perceives the person. This is precisely what results in the phenomenon of **preferential attachment** that we discussed in Principle 8, where success breeds success. Everyone wants to be attached to the best brands, people, and concepts, and so if you project an image of success, people will perceive you as being successful, and you will become a magnet for capital, connections, and additional accolades. The bigger and better everyone believes you are, the bigger and better you can be.

After I joined a larger firm, I learned that most brand name funds have brand names because they spend hundreds of thousands of dollars with PR firms who carefully cultivate an image of effortless achievement. Publicists leverage their relationships with reporters to place deliberately timed announcements about their clients who just closed their biggest fund ever, even if it actually took three years to raise and was legally closed 18 months ago. Or that one of the firm's portfolio companies raised a huge round of funding, or that one of their general partners is testifying in Congress on a key policy issue that is likely to benefit their investments in some way. As a peer, all you read is the headline, and you almost can't help but immediately get thrown into a cycle of "compare and despair." The clean story in the press is far from the messy reality, but it is all the VCs involved want you to know because industry veterans know what game they are playing. In the game of venture, what you *think* happened ultimately matters more to future results than whatever *actually* happened.

On the flip side, offering any hint of defeat can be a self-fulfilling prophecy. If you admit that you are not absolutely crushing it all the time or that you harbor doubts about your own potential, people will perceive you as unsuccessful and therefore not likely to be successful in the future. As a result, they will be less interested in investing their time and reputation with you. After all, your failure might also taint their ability to manifest their own success.

If nobody believes you will make it, you might never even get the chance.

> If you admit that you are not absolutely crushing it all the time or that you harbor doubts about your own potential, people will perceive you as unsuccessful and therefore not likely to be successful in the future.

Although authentic vulnerability has been a powerful way of forging meaningful connections in other parts of my life, I eventually came to understand that it could be counterproductive to my goals in venture capital. I hope this book plays a small part in normalizing more open, honest conversations about how challenging building a successful career in technology and venture capital can be. In the meantime, understanding the science behind *why* projecting an image of success works helped me come to peace with the fact that it is not always a smart strategy to share your deep insecurities with people who might not know you well enough to contextualize those doubts in the overall picture of your merits. This doesn't mean you're not being genuine; it means you recognize how venture capital works.

CREATE BENCHMARKS FOR YOUR PROCESS

We learned from the experts in network science that when performance can't be measured, networks drive success. The truth is that performance in venture capital *can* be measured, but it takes a very, very long time, and the result never becomes publicly available (unless you want it to). It can take decades to finalize performance numbers in each fund, yet most venture capital firms launch new funds every three years.

There are key benchmarks to measure fund performance (see sidebar, "The Measurement of Fund Performance"), and you should absolutely be tracking these metrics on a real-time basis, but they are not necessarily good indicators of whether or not you are spending your time on the right things. Why? These metrics fluctuate significantly over time because they tend to get skewed by large outcomes or significant write-downs. They're also not intuitive. You can read them on a piece of paper, but you can't *feel* or *sense* them. They are also heavily influenced by factors beyond your control as an investor, such as timing, market conditions, interest rates, the rest of your teammates, or fund size, to name a few. And they're really boring! For all of these reasons, they're not the best way to gauge how you are doing on a daily or weekly basis.

THE MEASUREMENT OF FUND PERFORMANCE

Fund performance is ultimately evaluated on:

- **IRR (internal rate of return).** A complex calculation meant to measure how efficiently you have invested your capital. This same metric can be applied to any type of investing, which in theory should allow investors to compare "apples to apples" across asset classes. Anything above 30 percent is considered to be very good.

- **MOIC (multiple on invested capital).** A venture-capital-specific benchmark measuring the markup on the money you have already deployed into companies, ignoring any amount that you have reserved or not yet invested. Anything within the range of 3x to 5x is considered to be very good.

- **TVPI (total value to paid in capital).** A venture-capital-specific benchmark measuring both the realized and unrealized value of a portfolio divided by the total amount of money you raised from investors (e.g., your total fund size). This benchmark only becomes relevant after most of the capital raised from investors has been deployed, often more than five years after a fund is launched.

- **DPI (distributed to paid-in capital).** A venture-capital-specific benchmark representing realized value on a fund. In other words, it is measuring how much money you have actually paid out to investors relative to how much they invested in the first place. Likely only relevant after seven or more years of a fund life.

However, learning to benchmark your own success is a powerful strategy for keeping yourself on course. Setting goals, measuring results, and iterating on your craft is an essential ingredient in any winning formula; it is also helpful to ensure you don't get lost in the sea of finely tuned projections of perfection that blanket the tech media on a daily basis. Furthermore, the world of venture is a roller coaster of emotions—it can take years to build a company and only a few months for it to disappear or suffer irrevocable losses. There will inevitably be regulatory inquiries, employee scandals, and competitive takeovers. If you get too hung up on one outcome, you'll lose sight of your long-term goals.

During my conversation with Joe Floyd, general partner at Emergence Capital, he shared how he learned to manage his mindset in a way that allowed him to stay the course long enough to put a win on the scoreboard. He told me that when he first joined Emergence Capital in 2012, his first investment was in a company called Salesloft, a software business focused on—you guessed it— salespeople. The product was okay, but his thesis was mostly around the founding team, who he believed to be exceptional entrepreneurs with a decent product that was showing early signs of success in the market. "A month after we invested," he recalled," we got a cease-and-desist letter from LinkedIn effectively killing our product. We had to totally start over."

Rocked by the fact that his first investment had gone south so quickly, Joe was devastated. "If I had just focused on my emotions, I would have gotten totally lost and given up. Luckily, my team helped me move forward by encouraging me to focus on the metrics I could control. They asked me every day, 'Are you working on three thesis areas that you think will lead to a great investment? Are you talking to a new entrepreneur every day?' They emphasized that if I stuck to the metrics I could control, they would eventually yield good results." Not only has Joe gone on to make a lot of great investments since that initial cease-and-desist letter, but the second iteration of product at Salesloft also ended up growing to $100 million in ARR (annualized run rate), and the company sold to Vista Equity Partners for $2.3 billion in 2021. It took nine years from the time he initially invested, but it was worth the wait.

It takes a long time to see what will happen with a specific company (nine years in the case of Salesloft), and each individual outcome is often a result of millions of factors, data points, and decisions. Many of those are completely impossible to predict or influence, no matter how good you are. Plus, venture capital business models are built to withstand a lot of failures. Short-term success can only be managed by measuring your process. Focus on identifying benchmarks tied to your process of accessing, analyzing, and adding value to your investments. Here are some of the ways in which I keep myself on track:

ACCESSING GREAT INVESTMENTS

- **How much time am I spending focused on sourcing high-quality deal flow?** I aim to spend at least 50 percent of my time meeting or cultivating relationships that lead to meeting founders about new potential investments.

- **How many entrepreneurs am I meeting every week?** I aim to meet entrepreneurs representing at least 40 new companies every month, which is 10 every week, or approximately 2 per day. This does not include reviewing business plans or decks from entrepreneurs I then decline to meet, of which there are probably an additional 10 to 15 per week.

- **What percentage of my meetings do I leave wanting to know more?** Meetings that don't lead anywhere are not very useful. This metric also serves as a way of assessing if I am sourcing investments in the right places. If I meet 40 new companies per month, I aim to dive deeper with at least 10 of them.

- **Am I finding at least two or three compelling opportunities every month?** A typical venture fund deployment cycle is two-and-a-half to three years. If you aim to make about 30 investments per fund, that is roughly 10 to 15 investments per year, or 1 per month. For every three companies I do deep diligence on (defined as three or more meetings), I expect to invest in one. Therefore, I want to be doing deep diligence on at least three companies per month.

ANALYZING POTENTIAL PORTFOLIO COMPANIES

- **What percentage of companies that I am doing diligence on do I end up investing in?** If my process is working, I will invest in one out of every three companies where I complete this entire process.

- **How many companies do I start diligence on and ultimately decline to invest?** I want to ensure that I am able to change my mind as I gain more information about a company. This should imply that my diligence process is thorough.

- **Am I winning the investments I am choosing?** I want to win 100 percent of the deals that I endeavor to invest in. This is not always realistic, but it is my personal goal for success.

ADDING VALUE TO EXISTING INVESTMENTS

- **How often am I meeting with founders whose companies are in my portfolio?** After I invest in a company, I aim to meet the founder at least monthly for the first six months, and every other month after that. In each meeting, I check in, ask what they are struggling with, and ask how I can help. I also come to the table with two or three ideas for how I can help move their business forward.

- **Have I identified a key metric for success?** Every investment is different, so in these first post-investment meetings, I work with founders to define what we are optimizing for. What is their number one metric for success this quarter? What are at least two or three ways I can help move the bar forward toward that success?

- **Have I expanded their network of customers and advisors?** Have I made at least three to five introductions for them this month? Have they proven to be productive?

- **How are their business metrics performing?** Although they are personally out of my control, we track financial results from our portfolio companies on a quarterly basis so that we can measure the impact of our efforts on their results, which include:

  - **Revenue growth.** How much money are they making this quarter versus last quarter, and also now versus the same time last year? How are they performing versus their revenue projections?

  - **Gross margin.** Revenue minus cost of goods sold, a typical measurement of how profitable a business is on a unit economics basis.

  - **Burn rate.** How much more money is the company spending than it is earning per month (income minus expenses)?

  - **Implied runway.** How many months until they run out of cash, or how many months until they will need to raise more money?

Take the time to create these benchmarks for yourself. Set bite-sized goals for where you'd like to be, and actively track your progress toward them on a monthly or a weekly basis. This is a helpful way of making long-term success more accessible, as well as a useful reminder to celebrate the small things. However, when it comes to goals, don't just set them and forget them and then expect you are on track for long-term wins to magically appear down the road. Incorporating introspection and regular reflection on whether your goals are the right ones is also a critical part of the process. Remember, we change over time, as do our motivations, priorities, and goals. Most teams do quarterly off-sites to assess progress as a firm. I also do a personal quarterly off-site to take time away from the daily grind and take stock of my situation. Although it may feel impossible to focus on the positive when objective performance takes so long to measure, taking a deliberate approach to measuring your advancement and relishing in successful execution of your process makes it a lot easier to focus on the positive.

> Incorporating introspection and regular reflection on whether your goals are the right ones is also a critical part of the process.

Jomayra Herrera, general partner at Reach Capital, follows this methodology as well. When I asked her how she would advise new investors to stay the course, she emphasized, "Relish in the small wins, otherwise you will burn out. I get my dopamine hits from making a helpful introduction, or I get a nice note from a founder about how I've added value to them. I see these as essential little wins that will eventually build into something big."

STEP 3

LOOK FOR COLLABORATORS, NOT ROLE MODELS

During our last fundraise, I met with a limited partner who was interested in investing several million dollars into our venture firm. He asked me, "What other venture firms or investors do you look up to? Who do you want to emulate?" I was both surprised and impressed by the depth and intimacy of the question, and suddenly I found myself racking my brains for a role model I admired, only to come up embarrassingly short on examples. Instead I remembered an interview I had recently watched on YouTube when a sports media outlet called Trans World Sport flew to Florida to interview then emerging stars 11-year-old Serena Williams and 12-year-old Venus Williams, who were just starting to make waves in the world of tennis. When the reporter asked Serena, "If you were going to be a tennis player [when you grow up], who would you want to be like?" Without skipping a beat, Serena smiled ear-to-ear and said, "Well, I'd like other people to be like me."[2] Serena was undaunted by the fact that were no other professional tennis players at the time who came from Compton, California, or from an African American background like she and her sister. Instead of wasting her time trying to be like someone else, Serena simply and eloquently captured the power of paving her own path forward without the luxury of having a role model that she could relate to dictating what her path should look like.

For anyone interested in breaking into venture capital but struggling to find a success story that they'd like to emulate, I encourage you to stop looking. Historically, venture capital has been an apprenticeship industry, meaning if you were just getting started, you were expected to learn on the job. Most firms operated on a model where the more seasoned partners would take new members of the team under their proverbial wing, transferring their knowledge over time by including the newbies in their process where they were expected to absorb the unwritten rules of the game. Some people are lucky in finding these types of mentors right off the bat. It is certainly a lot easier if a mentor can see him- or herself in you, but that isn't always the case if you look a little bit different or come from a different background than the previous generation of venture investors.

Whether or not there is someone already waiting in the wings to teach you the ropes, it is still tempting to seek a role model who has followed a pathway that might work for you as well. However, we have already established that it takes 10 or more years to validate objective success in venture, and even then you may not know for sure what an individual's performance metrics are. We also know that due to preferential attachment, it is much easier to continue to be successful once you are already successful. If you are just starting out, you may need to employ different tactics than those who have already "made it" so that you can get those early wins on the scoreboard. Finally, the industry is changing rapidly, and the current landscape of venture capital is far different than what it looked like 10 years ago, so if someone has already "made it," what worked for them might not work for you.

Instead of seeking out role models to emulate, find people to collaborate with you—people that may not necessarily define success for you, but instead will participate in it alongside you. For example, people who will:

* Make introductions to high-quality connectors within their network

* Invite you to coinvest in companies where they have high conviction

* Trade notes on due diligence, and even share resources they consulted in their process

* Serve as a reference for potential LPs as well as founders you may be interested in investing in

* Share their unfiltered perspectives on how they are navigating the industry and what may or may not be working for them

These are the types of people who will ultimately help you succeed, not just because you can and should, but also because the more you collaborate with someone, the more your success becomes intertwined. While "mentorship" implies that someone is helping you out of the goodness of their heart, and "role model" implies they may or may not know that you exist, collaborators are highly incentivized to help you because helping you simultaneously serves them. When we talk about the fact that success breeds success, it applies not just to your own success, but also the success of those around you.

STEP 4

JUST KEEP GOING

There is one guaranteed way to fail at venture capital—quit. In fact, I have almost quit venture capital exactly three times. One time, I went so far as to draft a business plan and lay the groundwork for starting a company instead. There were a variety of reasons why I thought I might not be meant to be a venture capitalist, but a key element of my frustration was that I didn't know if I was any good at it yet. Eventually, constant criticism and cutdowns from the people that were supposed to be supporting me had started to wear me down. Plus, my deep-seated desire to achieve was thwarted by the fact that objective success felt eternally out of reach (patience is not a strong suit of mine). In other words, I wanted to *win*. Even though years had passed since tip-off, it still felt like the game had only just begun. I wouldn't know if I had won until it was over . . . and as long as you keep going, it's never quite over. When you look at the glass half full, though, it means you always have another chance to throw the winning shot.

There is one guaranteed way to
fail at venture capital—quit.

The first time I nearly quit was when I had just moved to Tokyo and we were raising our second fund at Fresco Capital. We were hearing no from every investor we spoke to, and many of them were not delicate about it. We heard every excuse in the book, and the reality was that many of them were justified given that we were still early in our journey as investors and our strategy was unproven. It didn't help that I had recently called off an engagement to be married and was running very low on personal cash, not to mention self-confidence. My two partners, Tytus Michalski and Stephen Forte, were visiting

Japan for a multiday off-site where we were bouncing between coffee shops and restaurants, strategizing our path forward. As we walked out of a Starbucks into a sunny and perfectly clear Tokyo spring day, I sighed and looked up at the blue sky peeking between the skyscrapers. I could feel the exhausting weight of rejection bearing down on me. I shifted my gaze down to the sidewalk and shook my head. "Can we really build a venture capital firm? I don't know if it's in the cards for us," I said to my partners, wondering aloud if all of the naysayers were right to question us.

Steve, who is a confident and outspoken entrepreneur-turned-VC, grabbed both of my shoulders and turned me around to look him squarely in the eyes. He said, "Allison, I am going to teach you the most important phrase you will ever learn in your life and your career as an entrepreneur and investor. Are you ready for it?" I rolled my eyes and nodded, and he threw both arms up into the air, shook his fists at the sky, and exclaimed, "Fuck those fucking motherfuckers!"

He stepped back toward me and lifted my hands in the air, forcing me to say it with him. "Fuck those fucking motherfuckers!" I was whispering at first, but Steve kept egging me on. "Louder! Say it like you mean it!" he insisted. As my embarrassment waned and my confidence grew, I could feel my energy returning. Soon we were shaking our fists together, alarming innocent pedestrians all the way around the block.

Steve reminded me that we were in the business of funding things that literally had never been done before. And as a globally distributed team without brand-name investing experience and a young woman living in Japan as a general partner, we were also doing it in a way that had never been done before. Given those facts, of course people would question our ability to build a venture capital firm. However, we could choose whether or not to listen to them. The only thing that ultimately mattered was our ability to access, analyze, and add value to a few massive, world-changing companies. Every investment we made had the potential to generate unlimited upside for us and our investors—it would just take 10 years or more to figure out which ones were on that pathway. However, if we kept investing, we would maximize our chances of finding those one or two companies that would defy all odds and define our careers. If we gave up, stopped fundraising, and stopped making new investments, we would lose all chances of winning and proving everyone wrong. After all, you miss 100 percent of the shots you don't take.

I had early illusions that being a venture capitalist meant always being the one with the power to say yes or no. Although that is sometimes the case, the reality is that hearing no from others, whether they are limited partners, coinvestors, or entrepreneurs, is also a big part of the job. For someone who is highly motivated by achievement and the desire to win, a continuous stream of hearing no and failing is an acutely painful combination. Without the proper framework (and network of support) for managing this pain, it can become too much to bear. When I feel like I'm reaching that threshold, I think back to what it felt like to throw my hands up in the air in Tokyo that day, screaming, "Fuck those fucking motherfuckers!" at the top of my lungs and not caring who heard. Then I remember that to succeed, all I need to do is just keep going.

⸻

Breaking into venture capital is not about winning every time; it's about winning *when it matters*. The real skill is being able to figure out when it matters and to stay the course when it doesn't. Venture capital is the money that makes true innovation possible. It is a business of investing your time, energy, and resources in the impossible. With the right ingredients, the impossible embarks on a journey to the realm of the possible, then to the realm of reality, and then finally to the realm of ubiquity. That is a tall order, and most companies you invest in won't make it across the final threshold. But those that do will change the world, and you will know that you played a role in making that happen.

This book is intended to shed some light on how the game of venture capital gets played, but the most well-kept secret is that true success in venture capital is not achieved by following the rules. It does require figuring out what the rules are, but only so that you can bend them, break them, and rewrite them for future generations. Now, go get started!

BREAKTHROUGH TIPS
FOR STAYING THE COURSE

- Avoid focusing on what you read in the headlines. The game of venture capital requires projecting an image of success in order to attract more success, so there is a strong incentive to make winning look bigger, more lucrative, and easier than it really is.

- Identify who your close confidants are. Whether they are part of the industry or not, select a few people whom you can rely on to reflect your vulnerabilities and self-doubt back to you and help you learn from them without compromising your odds of success.

- Deliberately plan time on a quarterly basis to develop short-term, quantitative benchmarks that allow you to measure, iterate, and improve on your process for accessing, analyzing, and adding value to your investments.

- Build relationships with individuals who are not just interested in telling you what they did to be successful, but actually take action to support your progress toward these benchmarks.

- When you feel discouraged, prioritize continuing to make good investments to maximize your odds for long-term success.

GLOSSARY

Accelerator program. An education program that helps new companies grow faster by investing a small amount of money in exchange for equity, for example, $100,000 for 5 to 7 percent, and then providing structured support, advisory services, and a community for founders.

Angel investor. An individual investor in a startup, usually at the earliest stages.

Assets under management (AUM). The total amount of money handled by an investment firm across all funds.

B2B. Short for "business to business"; companies whose products or services are primarily purchased by other companies.

B2C. Short for "business to consumers"; companies whose products or services are primarily purchased by individuals.

Back channel influencers. People who are not explicitly recognized as decision makers but have the ability to impact a particular situation or outcome.

Back-channeling. Leveraging connections you have to influencers to sway a particular situation or outcome in a desired direction.

Blind introduction. When someone facilitates a connection without asking permission first.

Board of directors. The key governing body for a company charged with supervising the business, setting strategy, and making big decisions on behalf of the other shareholders, usually put in place at the time of the first priced equity round.

Burn rate. The amount of money a company is losing every month, calculated as income minus costs.

Business productivity. The output of a business relative to its costs.

Cap table (capitalization table). A document outlining the equity owners in a business as well as their percentage ownership.

Carried interest, or carry. The compensation tied to the success of an investment, typically 20 percent of profits after all initial capital is returned to investors.

Carveout. When investors proactively divert some of their returns to the founders and employees of a company.

CEO. Chief executive officer of a company, typically responsible for making all major business and strategic decisions. In the case of early stage startups, one of the cofounders is usually the CEO.

Churn. A term used to describe former customers that have stopped buying a product or service.

Cloud computing. The practice of using a network of remote servers instead of local servers to store and process data.

Coinvestors. Those who invest smaller amounts at the same terms as the lead investor.

Common shares. A security type typically reserved for founders and employees, paid out last in the event of a merger, acquisition, or liquidation and often with few or no voting rights.

Confirmation bias. A cognitive bias wherein individuals have already made up their mind and are merely searching for evidence to prove they are right.

Connectors. People who are highly incentivized to or enjoy introducing investors and startups.

Conversion milestones. A term in a convertible note that dictates when and how the loan will convert into equity.

Convertible note. A short-term loan that converts into equity upon a future financing, typically used to raise capital at the very early (pre-seed or seed) or very late (pre-IPO) stage of a company's life cycle.

Cultural zeitgeist. A distinct movement and sense of excitement and/or moment around a change in a specific cultural topic or issue.

Deal flow. A pipeline of potential investment opportunities.

Deal flow ROI. An analysis of how much deal flow has resulted from a specific investment of time, capital, or relationships.

Deep technology innovations. A new product or process where the technology itself is considered to be novel, regardless of how it is used—for example, quantum computing, self-guided artificial intelligence, new medical devices, or new pharmaceutical treatments.

Demographic shift. The phenomenon of a new generation gaining power, authority, and influence by becoming the majority of the workforce or owning the majority of consumer wallet share.

Dilution. A reduction in ownership resulting from the creation of additional equity shares.

DPI (distributed to paid-in capital). A venture-capital-specific benchmark representing realized value on a fund; in other words, it measures how much money you have actually paid out to investors relative to how much they invested.

Dry powder. Unallocated reserves in a venture capital fund.

Due diligence (DD). The process of analyzing each opportunity carefully and ultimately deciding whether or not to invest.

Early stage funds. Funds that focus on investing in companies that are pre-PMF (prior to assessment of product-market fit).

Early stage investing. Investing once an idea has turned into a real business with paying customers but when it is still only a few years old.

Economic shock. A sudden change in financial or business conditions as a result of a specific event.

Fiduciary duty. The legal obligation to act in the best interest of one's shareholders.

Follow-on capital. Dollars reserved at the time of an initial investment by an investor for future financing rounds if a company is proving to be successful.

Follow-on funding. An additional round of funding after the initial investment.

Founder. A person who establishes a new company.

Founder/market fit. A criteria used by investors to evaluate an investment opportunity by identifying whether or not founders have personal experience with the problem they are solving.

Growth stage investing. Investing in a proven business that can grow faster with additional capital.

Hard landing. Declaring bankruptcy or shutting down the company altogether. The opposite of a soft landing.

Headwinds. External factors that slow down a business by adding resistance to its natural path of growth.

Impostor syndrome. The belief that one does not deserve their position, despite their accomplishments or skill set.

Information rights. A term delineating who has access to key proprietary information about the company's performance.

Inheriting a portfolio. When someone joins a new investment firm and becomes part owner of a set of companies in which they did not necessarily make the decision to invest.

IPO (initial public offering). When a company sells equity to the public for the first time by listing on a public exchange.

Interest rate. The cost of capital, outlined in a convertible loan document, paid by the company to an investor, that accrues between the time of investment and a conversion milestone; often, the amount is not paid as cash but converted into additional equity at the predetermined milestone.

Investable. When an idea becomes a specific and actionable opportunity for deploying capital.

Investment thesis. A reasoned argument for a particular investment strategy, backed up by research and analysis.

IRR (internal rate of return). A complex calculation meant to measure how efficiently you have invested your capital; this same metric can be applied to any type of investing, which in theory should allow investors to compare "apples to apples" across asset classes.

Later stage funds. Funds that focus on investing in post-PMF growth (growth after assessment of product-market fit).

Lead investor. The investment firm or partner who sets the terms of the investment and typically takes a seat on the board of directors.

Liquidation preference. An investment term that outlines how and when you will get paid back in the event there is some sort of change in control (merger, acquisition, bankruptcy, or IPO) of the business before conversion occurs. A 1x liquidation preference means you get your money invested back before any other shareholders get their first dollar; 2x means you get twice your money back, and so on.

Loss aversion. A well-documented form of irrational decision motivated by the fact that individuals experience more pain from losing money than the joy they experience from gaining the same amount.

Management fee. An annual fee on the total amount of committed capital in a fund, paid by the limited partners to the general partner to cover costs of operating such as salaries, travel, and office space.

Market mapping. The process of learning about a specific market sector or landscape.

Marketplaces. Platforms that charge a transaction fee for matching buyers and sellers.

Maturity date. The predetermined date outlined in a convertible note when the loan will convert into equity.

MOIC (multiple on invested capital). A venture-capital-specific benchmark measuring the markup on the money you have already deployed into companies, ignoring any amount that you have reserved or not yet invested.

Negativity bias. The human brain's tendency to remember bad experiences more acutely than good experiences.

Opting in. Choosing to participate in something, more specifically the act of expressing interest in being connected with someone.

Ownership stake. The percentage of a company's equity that belongs to you after your investment.

Paper gain. An increase in the value of your ownership stake that has not yet resulted in a cash return on your investment.

Post-money valuation. How much the company is worth once the financing is complete. This is important because the cash raised as part of the investment is considered an asset, and therefore adds to the equity value of the business. It can be calculated by adding the pre-money valuation and the investment round size.

Postmortem. The process of analyzing an investment or a choice you made after the ultimate result has been determined.

Power law. A mathematic concept describing how companies with exponential growth have an outsized impact on portfolio returns, rendering all other investments in the portfolio relatively meaningless.

Preferred shares. A security type usually created for investors during a financing round that includes special voting rights and getting paid out first among equity holders in the event of a liquidation.

Pre-money valuation. How much the company is worth at the time of the financing, before taking into account the cash it will receive as part of the investment round.

Pre-seed or seed funds. Funds that focus on providing funding before the product or business actually exists.

Pre-seed investing. Investing in a team and an idea before they have any customers or product.

Priced equity round. A formal financing round that creates new equity shares that are issued to investors at the time of financing based on a predetermined equity valuation and share price.

Product-market fit (PMF). Concrete evidence that customers want what a company is selling and are willing to pay for it in a predictable way.

Qualified financing. A term for an investment round, often used as a conversion milestone, that involves another fundraising event of a designated size.

Reserves. Dollars set aside in a fund for future follow-on investments in existing portfolio companies.

ROI (return on investment). Calculation of how much of a desired output has resulted from a set amount of a given input (usually money or time).

Round size. How much money the company is raising in a given financing.

Runway. The number of months or years that a company can continue to grow unprofitably before running out of cash.

SAFE note. Stands for "Simple Agreement for Future Equity," a templatized convertible note created by the startup accelerator Y Combinator in 2013 to help founders standardize terms and ensure fair standards for early stage investments.

Security. A fungible, transferable financial instrument that represents some financial value, such as stocks, bonds, or loans.

Seed stage investing. Investing in a team, an idea, and a minimum viable product, which is the seed that gets planted and hopefully grows into a large, lucrative oak tree.

Series A. A financing round that occurs after a seed round, once a company has demonstrated sufficient product-market fit.

Series B. A growth round of financing that occurs after the Series A.

Series C. A larger, later growth round of financing that occurs after the Series B.

Social proof. A cognitive bias that occurs when you believe and trust that other people know something better than you do.

Soft landing. An exit, most commonly a merger or acquisition, that is not meaningfully financially for anyone involved, but helps a company, its product, and its founders find a new home and save face by being able to claim that they were acquired. The opposite of a hard landing.

Stage-agnostic. A willingness to invest at any point in a company life cycle.

Sunk cost fallacy. A cognitive bias where people believe that the amount of money or time they have already invested in something makes it inherently more valuable.

Super-connectors. People who pride themselves on making introductions within their network.

Tailwinds. External factors that benefit a startup's growth in a positive way, similar to how wind blowing in the direction of an aircraft helps increase its speed, regardless of the skill of the pilot.

Tall poppy syndrome. A term frequently used in New Zealand and Australia for criticizing someone for their accomplishments or unique attributes.

Term sheet. A proposal outlining the details of what investors are putting into a company, what they are getting in return, and how money flows back to shareholders in the case of an exit, a change in control, or a liquidation of the company.

TVPI (total value to paid-in capital). A venture-capital-specific benchmark measuring both the realized and unrealized value of a fund. Calculated by taking the amount that the investment portfolio is worth and dividing by the total amount of money raised from investors.

Valuation cap. A term in a convertible note that represents the maximum dollar amount used to calculate how much equity an investor will receive in exchange for their up-front cash investment.

Voting rights. A term dictating who votes on what and how many people need to vote yes for something to get approved, such as an acquisition offer, removing a CEO, etc.

NOTES

Introduction

1. As reported in the *New York Times*; it was their largest acquisition to date.
2. https://www.theinformation.com/articles/vc-pay-surged-again-in -2021-but-future-jumps-are-in-jeopardy?rc=61mzvl.
3. https://www.theinformation.com/articles/vc-pay-surged-again-in -2021-but-future-jumps-are-in-jeopardy?rc=61mzvl.
4. As measured by one- and three-year internal rate of return metrics (IRR). Source: Pitchbook Global Fund Performance Report, Q3 2020.
5. Source: Pitchbook-NVCA Venture Monitor, Q2 2021.
6. https://statisticstimes.com/economy/countries-by-gdp.php.
7. Source: *Vault Career Guide to Venture Capital*, 2021.
8. https://engineering.stanford.edu/about/heroes/2011-heroes/fred -terman.
9. https://steveblank.com/2009/04/27/the-secret-history-of-silicon -valley-part-vi-the-secret-life-of-fred-terman-and-stanford/.
10. https://ventureforward.org/education/history-101/.

Facts and Fundamentals

1. https://www.sec.gov/education/capitalraising/building-blocks/ accredited-investor.

Part One

1. https://www.gemconsortium.org/.
2. Randall Stross, *eBoys: The True Story of the Six Tall Men Who Backed eBay, Webvan, and Other Billion-Dollar Start-Ups* (Crown Business, 2000).
3. https://pitchbook.com/news/articles/2021-record-year-us-venture-capital-six-charts.
4. https://www.wsj.com/articles/SB886380588905280000.

Principle 1

1. https://www.moneyfactory.gov/images/4-_January_FY22_End_of_the_Month_Report_2-9-22.pdf.

Principle 2

1. https://www.amazon.com/Made-Stick-Ideas-Survive-Others/dp/1400064287.
2. https://www.businessinsider.com/dcm-blows-out-vc-competitors-with-30x-returns-investing-china-2021-7.
3. https://www.forbes.com/sites/zinnialee/2022/02/22/singapore-crypto-firm-amber-group-hits-3-billion-valuation-in-funding-round-led-by-temasek/?sh=747a6db534e4.
4. https://interactioninstitute.org/power-dynamics-the-hidden-element-to-effective-meetings/.

Principle 3

1. https://www.wsj.com/articles/SB10001424053111903480904576512250915629460.
2. https://medium.com/@allisonbaumgates/investing-in-the-future-of-work-eec30f6455e9.
3. https://www.epi.org/publication/understanding-the-historic-divergence-between-productivity-and-a-typical-workers-pay-why-it-matters-and-why-its-real/.
4. https://www.census.gov/topics/employment/labor-force.html.
5. https://www.mhanational.org/sites/default/files/Mind%20the%20Workplace%20-%20MHA%20Workplace%20Health%20Survey%202017%20FINAL.PDF.
6. https://www.economist.com/graphic-detail/2018/04/24/a-study-finds-nearly-half-of-jobs-are-vulnerable-to-automation.
7. https://www.pewresearch.org/fact-tank/2018/04/11/millennials-larg.
8. https://www.wsj.com/articles/SB10001424053111903480904576512250915629460.

9. https://medicalxpress.com/news/2016-12-american-death-drugs
   -alcohol-mental.html.
10. https://www.inc.com/minda-zetlin/most-americans-have-almost-no
    -savings-even-if-they-make-more-than-100000-a-yea.html.
11. https://www.mhanational.org/sites/default/files/Mind%20the%20
    Workplace%20-%20MHA%20Workplace%20Health%20Survey%
    202017%20FINAL.PDF.
12. https://files.pitchbook.com/website/files/pdf/Q1_2022_PitchBook
    _NVCA_Venture_Monitor.pdf#page=1.
13. https://files.pitchbook.com/website/files/pdf/Q1_2022_PitchBook
    _NVCA_Venture_Monitor.pdf#page=1.
14. https://techcrunch.com/2021/12/08/silicon-valleys-share-of-us-vc
    -funding-falls-to-lowest-level-in-more-than-a-decade/.
15. https://revolution.com/entity/rotr/.
16. https://www.cnbc.com/2021/03/25/sequoia-capital-india-announces
    -second-seed-fund-at-195-million.html.
17. https://femalefoundersfund.com/about/.

Part Two

1. https://www.bvp.com/anti-portfolio.

Principle 4

1. https://www.ted.com/talks/bill_gross_the_single_biggest_reason
   _why_start_ups_succeed.
2. *The Power Law*, page 16.
3. *The Power Law*, page 17.
4. https://www.bls.gov/oes/current/oes499064.htm.
5. https://learn.angellist.com/articles/safe-note.
6. https://www.pewresearch.org/fact-tank/2018/04/11/millennials
   -largest-generation-us-labor-force/.
7. https://www.who.int/news/item/02-03-2022-covid-19-pandemic
   -triggers-25-increase-in-prevalence-of-anxiety-and-depression
   -worldwide.

Principle 5

1. https://techcrunch.com/2018/06/18/bittorrent-tron/.

Principle 6

1. https://news.crunchbase.com/news/global-vc-funding-to-female
   -founders/.
2. http://about.crunchbase.com/wp-content/uploads/2020/10/2020
   _crunchbase_diversity_report.pdf.

3. https://www.wired.com/story/vc-pledged-better-diversity-its-barely
-changed/.
4. https://www.forbes.com/sites/elizabethedwards/2021/02/24/check
-your-stats-the-lack-of-diversity-in-venture-capital-is-worse-than-it
-looks/?sh=115a83c185de.

Principle 7

1. https://www.nytimes.com/2015/10/07/business/dealbook/silicon
-valley-still-lacks-diversity-study-shows.html.
2. https://www.newportinstitute.com/resources/mental-health/tall
-poppy-syndrome/.
3. https://static1.squarespace.com/static/5c44cad64eddeceaf51991b3/t/
5c7f30a5652dea9fd7d312bd/1551839408555/The+Tallest+Poppy
+Whitepaper.pdf.
4. https://www.nytimes.com/2015/10/07/business/dealbook/silicon
-valley-still-lacks-diversity-study-shows.html.

Principle 8

1. Tugend, Alina. "Praise is Fleeting but Brickbats We Recall." *New York Times*. (2012/03/24). https://www.nytimes.com/2012/03/24/
your-money/why-people-remember-negative-events-more-than
-positive-ones.html.
2. *The Power Law*, 17.
3. Albert-László Barabási, *The Formula: The Universal Laws of Success*, 109.
4. https://www.amazon.com/Put-Your-Strengths-Work-Outstanding/
dp/0743261682.

Principle 9

1. Albert-László Barabási, *The Formula*, 40.
2. https://www.youtube.com/watch?v=p31aGy_jD3E.

ACKNOWLEDGMENTS

I always knew I was going to write a book, I just didn't know when or what it would be about. Throughout the process, I was fascinated to learn how similar the publishing world is to that of venture capital. I owe a big thank you to everyone along the way who helped me access the right partners on this journey, analyze the best path forward, and ultimately (hopefully) add value to you, my readers. I am appreciative of all the agents, publishers, and friends who asked probing questions, pushed my thinking, and weren't afraid to give me direct feedback instead of just nodding, smiling, and ignoring me when I was missing the mark. I may not have liked hearing it at the time, but it made all the difference.

Thank you to Adele Barlow for pushing me and my writing over the years, and ultimately giving me the coaching and encouragement I needed to write the proposal and put myself out there. Thank you to my fellow author, Melissa Daimler, for opening up her network and connecting me to her partners at McGraw Hill. Of course, none of this would be possible without my incredible editor, Michele Matrisciani. I have learned so much from you. You pushed me to dig deeper into what I know, what I wanted to say, and who I wanted to say it to.

Thank you to Angela Lee and Dr. Kurt Byer for giving me the opportunity to teach alongside them at some of the world's best academic institutions, which enabled me to figure out what you really need to know about venture capital to succeed within it. You believed I had something to share with the next generation of investors, and that was a key ingredient in my ability to plow through my self-doubt to write this book.

Thank you to Tytus Michalski and Stephen Forte for taking a chance on me so many years ago in Hong Kong—you saw something in me that I didn't see in myself. You treated me as an equal from day one and it completely transformed my view of the business world. You were the most incredible business partners and people I could have ever asked for and I am so grateful that you were such a big part of my journey.

Thank you to my partners today, Robby Peters, Greg Golub, Caribou Honig, and Colin Tobias, as well as the rest of the team at SemperVirens for building such an exciting platform transforming the future of work and venture capital.

Thank you to my baby, Jackson, for (literally) being the fire in my belly to get this done on schedule. Thank you, Mom, for loving and encouraging me and my writing over the years. It was only because of you that I was miraculously able to give birth and finish this manuscript in the same month.

Finally, thank you to Jason for being the best partner I could ever ask for. From the moment you brought discussion notes on my future of work thesis to our first date, I knew I wanted to invest in forever with you. Your questions, insights, and encouragement make me a better person and a better investor every day.

INDEX

ABOUT THE AUTHOR

ALLISON BAUM GATES is a general partner at SemperVirens Venture Capital, an early stage fund investing in technology transforming the future of work. She is also a writer, speaker, adjunct assistant professor at Columbia Business School, lecturer at UC Berkeley, wife to Jason, mom to Jackson, and dog mom to Ace. A native of Illinois, she has lived and worked in Boston, New York, Paris, Hong Kong, Tokyo, and San Francisco. *Breaking into Venture* is her first book. Connect with her at allisonbaumgates.com.